COINS OF ENGLAND

& THE UNITED KINGDOM

DECIMAL ISSUES
STANDARD CATALOGUE OF BRITISH COINS
PART 3

SPINK

LONDON

A Catalogue of the Decimal Coins of Great Britain
and Ireland

Standard Catalogue of British Coins
Coins of England and the United Kingdom
1st edition, 2015

© Spink & Son Ltd, 2014
69 Southampton Row, Bloomsbury
London WC1B 4ET

Typeset by Design to Print UK Ltd,
9 & 10 Riverview Business Park, Forest Row, East Sussex RH18 5DW
www.designtoprintuk.com
Printed and bound in Malta by
Gutenberg Press Ltd.

ISBN 978-1-907427-44-2

CONTENTS

ACKNOWLEDGEMENTS

We wish to acknowledge the valuable contributions of the following who have submitted information and provided photographs which have greatly enhanced this edition.

Kevin Clancy, *Royal Mint*
Paul Davies
David Fletcher
Andrew Jenkins, *Royal Mint*
Geoff Kitchen
Kerry Willecome, *Royal Mint*

FOREWORD

Welcome to the first edition of the new Coins of England Decimal Issues, we hope you enjoy this new volume which has been promised for the last few years. It is a happy coincidence that the release of this new edition appears at the same time that we issue the 50th edition of the main Coins of England volume so it is a landmark year for the catalogue.

The decision to create a separate book has been driven by several factors, the main reason being that the volume of new issues coming from the Royal Mint has dramatically increased the size of the main Coins of England book and the compact nature of that volume was being compromised. There will obviously continue to be many new issues from the Royal Mint in the future so, in order to continue listing all of these new issues, we felt we had to migrate the Decimal Coinage to its own volume where it can benefit from the addition of new illustrations and new information as we work more closely with the Royal Mint to obtain as much accurate information as possible. The book retains the same format and numbering system as before but we intend to re-number and re-arrange the catalogue in future editions to create a more user friendly layout.

The prices in the catalogue represent the range of retail prices at which coins are being offered for sale at the time of going to press and NOT the price which a dealer will pay. These prices are based on our knowledge of the market and the current demand for particular coins. Where prices have not been given it is usually because they are very recent issues and a price has not yet been established for the secondary market. In many cases the precious metal content of the coin is a major factor in deciding the value so the price of many coins will fluctuate with the value of the metal content.

As always, we welcome suggestions from users to make this catalogue more accurate and user-friendly so please feel free to write to us at Spink with your comments.

Happy collecting

Philip Skingley
Editor, Coins of England

INTRODUCTION

The decision to adopt decimal currency was announced in March 1966 following the recommendation of the Halsbury Committee of Enquiry which had been appointed in 1961. The date for the introduction of the new system was 15 February 1971 and it was evident that the Royal Mint facilities which had been located on Tower Hill for more than 150 years would be unable to strike the significant quantities of coins required on that site. The Government therefore decided to build a new mint at Llantrisant in South Wales.

The new system provided for three smaller bronze coins with the denominations of a half new penny, one new penny and two new pence, and very large numbers were struck and stock piled for D-Day. The cupro-nickel five and ten new pence denominations with the same specifications as the shilling and florin were introduced in 1968 and circulated along side the former denominations. A further change was the introduction in 1969 of a 50 new pence coin to replace the ten shilling banknote.

In 1982 and 1983 two more new coins were introduced; the 20 pence which helped to reduce demand for five and ten pence pieces, and the first circulating non-precious metal £1 coin which replaced the bank note of the same value.1982 also saw the removal of the word "NEW" from all denominations from half penny to fifty pence.

Increasing raw material costs, and inflation also play a part in the development of a modern coinage system and smaller 5 and 10 pence coins were introduced in 1990 and 1992 respectively. A further change in 1992 was the use of copper plated steel for the one and two pence bronze coins. The plated steel coins are magnetic unlike the solid bronze alloy. Further changes were made in 1997 when the fifty pence coin was reduced in size and a bimetallic circulating £2 was also introduced to reduce demand for the one pound value.

In 2008, 40 years after the introduction of the first of the decimal coin designs, a completely new series was issued. After an open competition that attracted more than 4,000 entries, designs by a young graphic designer, Matthew Dent, were selected, and represent a somewhat radical approach that uses elements of the shield of the Royal Arms for the denominations of 50 pence to 1 pence. The £1 shows the complete shield. Interestingly none of the coins show the value in numerical form.

The Mint offered sets of the new designs in various metals and qualities, and also gave collectors an opportunity to acquire the last issues of the original series. These, together with various commemorative issues, present collectors with a significant and varied range, and illustrate the importance of the sales of special issues to the Mint's business.

In the 40 years since Decimalisation there have been changes to the obverse portrait of Her Majesty The Queen with the exception of the Silver Maundy coins which retain the Mary Gillick design. The new effigy for the introduction of the decimal series was by Arnold Machin, followed then by Raphael Maklouf, and the current portrait is by Ian Rank - Broadley.

Previous editions of the catalogue listed coins according to the portrait rather than by denomination. After discussion with dealers and contributors, it has been decided that a radical change should be made so that users of the catalogue can see all issues of a particular denomination in sequence, starting with the lowest value and progressing to the highest. This will help collectors of, for example, £1, £2 and crown size coins. Catalogue numbers have been retained from the previous edition.

BRONZE

Obverse portrait by Arnold Machin

4239   4240

4239 Half new penny. R. The Royal Crown and the inscription '1/2 NEW PENNY'
(Reverse design: Christopher Ironside)

1971......................£0.50	1975............................£0.50	1979..........................£0.50
— Proof *FDC** £1	— Proof *FDC** £1	— Proof *FDC** £1
1972 Proof *FDC** £2	1976............................£0.50	1980..........................£0.50
1973......................£0.50	— Proof *FDC** £1	— Proof *FDC** £1
— Proof *FDC** £1	1977............................£0.50	1981..........................£0.50
1974......................£0.50	— Proof *FDC** £1	— Proof *FDC** £1
— Proof *FDC** £1	1978............................£0.50	
	— Proof *FDC** £1	

4240 Half penny. 'New' omitted. As illustration

1982...............£0.50	1983............................£0.50	1984*..............................£2
— Proof *FDC** £1	— Proof *FDC** £1	— Proof *FDC**..........£2

Obverse portrait by Arnold Machin

4237   4238   4381

4237 One new penny. R. A portcullis with chains royally crossed, being the badge of Henry
VII and his successors, and the inscription 'NEW PENNY' above and the figure '1' below.
(Design: Christopher Ironside)

1971......................£0.50	1975............................£0.50	1979..........................£0.50
— Proof *FDC** £1	— Proof *FDC** £1	— Proof *FDC**..........£1
1972 Proof *FDC** £2	1976............................£0.50	1980..........................£0.50
1973......................£0.50	— Proof *FDC** £1	— Proof *FDC** £1
— Proof *FDC** £1	1977............................£0.50	1981..........................£0.50
1974......................£0.50	— Proof *FDC** £1	— Proof *FDC** £1
— Proof *FDC** £1	1978............................£0.50	
	— Proof *FDC** £1	

4238 One penny. 'New' omitted, As illustration

1982...............£0.50	1983............................£0.50	1984...............................£1
— Proof *FDC** £1	— *FDC** £1	— Proof *FDC**..........£1

Obverse portrait by Raphael Maklouf

4381 One penny. R. Crowned portcullis with chains

1985......................£0.50	1988............................£0.50	1991..........................£0.50
— Proof *FDC** £1	— Proof *FDC** £1	— Proof *FDC**...........£1
1986......................£0.50	1989............................£0.50	1992..........................£0.50
— Proof *FDC** £1	— Proof *FDC** £1	— Proof *FDC** £1
1987......................	1990	
— Proof *FDC** £1	— Proof *FDC** £1	

* Coins marked thus were originally issued in Royal Mint sets.

COPPER PLATED STEEL

4391 **One penny** R. Crowned portcullis with chains

1992 .... £0.50	1995 .... £0.50	1997 .... £0.50
1993 .... £0.50	— Proof *FDC** £1	— Proof *FDC** £1
— Proof *FDC** £1	1996 .... £0.50	
1994 .... £0.50	— Proof *FDC** £1	
— Proof *FDC** £1	— Proof in silver *FDC**£15	

Obverse portrait by Ian Rank-Broadley

4710

4710 **One penny.** R. Crowned portcullis with chains. (Illus. as 4381)

1998 .... £1	2004 .... £1
— Proof *FDC* * £3	— Proof *FDC** £3
1999 .... £1	2005 .... £1
— Proof *FDC* * £3	— Proof *FDC** £3
2000 .... £1	2006 .... £1
— Proof *FDC* * £3	— Proof *FDC** £3
— Proof in silver FDC (see PSS08)* £8	— Proof in silver *FDC* (see PSS22)* ... £8
2001 .... £1	2007 .... £1
— Proof *FDC* * £3	— Proof *FDC* * £3
2002 .... £1	2008 .... £1
— Proof *FDC* * £3	— Proof *FDC* * £3
— Proof in gold *FDC* (see PGJS1)*£200	— Proof in silver *FDC* (see PSS27)* ... £8
2003 .... £1	— Proof in gold *FDC* (see PGEBCS)*£225
— Proof *FDC* * £3	— Proof in platinum *FDC*
	(see PPEBCS)* £300

4711

4711 **One penny.** R. A section of Our Royal Arms showing elements of the first and third quartering accompanied by the words 'ONE PENNY'(Reverse design: Matthew Dent)

2008 .... £3
— Proof *FDC* (in 2008 set, see PS96)* £3
— Proof in silver *FDC* (in 2008 set, see PSS28)* £8
— Proof piedfort in silver *FDC* (in 2008 set, see PSS29)* £15
— Proof in gold *FDC* (in 2008 set, see PGRSAS)* £225
— Proof in platinum *FDC* (in 2008 set, see PPRSAS)* £300
2009
— Proof *FDC* (in 2009 set, see PS97)*
— BU in silver £15
— Proof in silver *FDC* (in 2009 set, see PSS 37)* £15

* Coins marked thus were originally issued in Royal Mint sets.

2010
—   Proof *FDC* (in 2010 set, see PS101)* £3
—   BU in silver £15
—   Proof in silver *FDC* (in 2010 set, Edition: 3,500, see PSS41)* £15
2011 .... £3
—   Proof *FDC* (in 2011 set, see PS104) * £3
—   BU in silver... £15
—   Proof in silver *FDC* (in 2011 set, Edition: 2,500, see PSS44)* £15
2012 .... £3
—   Proof *FDC* (in 2012 set, see PS107) * £3
—   BU in silver... £23
—   Proof in silver *FDC* (Edition: 995, see PSS47)* £30
—   Proof in silver with selected gold plating *FDC* (Edition: 2,012, see PSS48) * £30
—   Proof in gold *FDC* (Edition: 150 see PGDJS)* £225
2013 .... £3
—   Proof *FDC* (in 2013 set, see PS109)* £5
—   BU in silver £23
—   Proof in silver *FDC* (Edition: 2,013, see PSS50)* £30
—   Proof in gold *FDC* (Edition: 60 see PGCAS)* £225
2014 .... £5
—   Proof *FDC* (in 2014 set, see PS112)*
—   Proof in silver *FDC* (Edition: 2014 see PSS56)*

BRONZE

Obverse portrait by Arnold Machin

    4235   4236

4235 Two new pence. R. The badge of the Prince of Wales, being three ostrich feathers enfiling a coronet of cross pattee and fleur de lys, with the motto 'ICH DIEN', and the inscription '2 NEW PENCE' (Reverse design: Christopher Ironside)

1971..................... £0.50	1976 ....£0.50	1979..........................£0.50
— Proof *FDC*...... £1	— Proof *FDC* £1	— Proof *FDC*...........£1
1972 Proof *FDC*...... £2	1977 ....£0.50	1980..........................£0.50
1973 Proof *FDC*...... £2	— Proof *FDC* £1	— Proof *FDC*...........£1
1974 Proof *FDC*...... £2	1978 ....£0.50	1981..........................£0.50
1975..................... £0.50	— Proof *FDC* £1	— Proof *FDC*...........£1
— Proof *FDC*....... £1		

4236 Two pence. 'New' omitted. As illustration

1982*...........................£1	1983*...........................£1	1984*...........................£1
— Proof *FDC*....... £2	— Proof *FDC* £2	— Proof *FDC*...........£2

4236A — Error reverse. The word 'new' was dropped from the reverse of the currency issues in 1982 but a number of 2 pence coins were struck in 1983 with the incorrect reverse die, similar to coins listed as 4235. Reports suggest that the error coins, or 'Mules' were contained in some sets packed by the Royal Mint for Martini issued in 1983 .... £750

* Coins marked thus were originally issued in Royal Mint sets.

Obverse portrait by Raphael Maklouf

4376

4376 Two pence. R. Prince of Wales feathers

1985......................£0.50	1988.............................£0.50	1991...........................£0.50
— Proof *FDC**........£1	— Proof *FDC** £1	— Proof *FDC**...........£1
1986......................£0.50	1989.............................£0.50	1992...........................£0.50
— Proof *FDC**........£1	— Proof *FDC** £1	— Proof *FDC**...........£1
1987......................£0.50	1990.............................£0.50	
— Proof *FDC**........£1	— Proof *FDC** £1	

COPPER PLATED STEEL

4386 Two pence R. Plumes

1992...........................£1	1995..................................£1	1997...........................£0.50
1993...........................£1	— Proof *FDC** £1	— Proof *FDC** £1
— Proof *FDC** £1	1996..................................£1	
1994...........................£1	— Proof *FDC** £1	
— Proof *FDC**........£1	— Proof in silver *FDC**£15	

Obverse portrait by Ian Rank-Broadley

4690

4690 Two pence. R. Prince of Wales feathers.

1998...£1	2004 ....£1
— Proof *FDC** £3	— Proof *FDC** £3
1999...£1	2005 ....£1
— Proof *FDC** £3	— Proof *FDC** £3
2000...£1	2006 ....£1
— Proof *FDC** £3	— Proof *FDC** £3
— Proof in silver FDC (see PSS08)* £8	— Proof in silver *FDC* (see PSS22)* £8
2001...£1	2007 ....£1
— Proof *FDC** £3	— Proof *FDC** £3
2002...£1	2008 ....£1
— Proof *FDC** £3	— Proof *FDC** £3
— Proof in gold *FDC* (see PGJS1)*£400	— Proof in silver *FDC* (see PSS27)* £10
2003	— Proof in gold *FDC* (see PGEBCS)* ...£450
— Proof *FDC** £3	— Proof in platinum *FDC*
	(see PPEBCS)* £550

* Coins marked thus were originally issued in Royal Mint sets.

4691

4691 Two pence. R. A section of Our Royal Arms showing elements of the second quartering
accompanied by the words 'TWO PENCE'(Reverse design: Matthew Dent)
2008 ....£3
—   Proof *FDC* (in 2008 set, see PS96)* £3
—   Proof in silver *FDC* (in 2008 set, see PSS28)* £10
—   Proof piedfort in silver *FDC* (in 2008 set, see PSS29)* £20
—   Proof in gold *FDC* (in 2008 set, see PGRSAS)* £450
—   Proof in platinum *FDC* (in 2008 set, see PPRSAS)*......................................£550
2009 ....£3
—   Proof *FDC* (in 2009 set, see PS97)* £3
—   Proof in silver *FDC* (in 2009 set, see PSS 37)* £10
2010 ....£3
—   Proof *FDC* (in 2010 set, see PS101)* £3
—   Proof in silver *FDC* (in 2010 set, Edition: 3,500 see PSS41)* £10
2011 ....£3
—   Proof *FDC* (in 2011 set, see PS104) * £3
—   Proof in silver *FDC* (in 2011 set, Edition: 2,500, see PSS44) * £15
2012 ....£3
—   Proof *FDC* (in 2012 set, see PS107) * £3
—   Proof in silver *FDC* (Edition: 995, see PSS47)*..£30
—   Proof in silver with selected gold plating *FDC* (Edition: 2,012, see PSS48) * £30
—   Proof in gold *FDC* (Edition: 150 see PGDJS)* £450
2013 ....£3
—   Proof *FDC* (in 2013 set, see PS110) * £5
—   Proof in silver *FDC* (Edition: 2,013, see PSS50)*..£30
—   Proof in gold *FDC* (Edition: 60 see PGCAS)* £450
2014 ....£3
—   Proof *FDC* (in 2014 set, see PS112) * £5
—   Proof in silver *FDC* (Edition : 2,014 see PSS56)*

* Coins marked thus were originally issued in Royal Mint sets.

CUPRO-NICKEL

Obverse portrait by Arnold Machin

4233   4234

4233 Five new pence. R. A thistle royally crowned, being the badge of Scotland, and the inscription '5 NEW PENCE' (Reverse design: Christopher Ironside)

1968...................... £0.50	1974 Proof *FDC** £4	1979..........................£0.50
1969...................... £0.50	1975 ....£0.50	— Proof *FDC**..........£2
1970...................... £0.50	— Proof *FDC** £2	1980..........................£0.50
1971...................... £0.50	1976 Proof *FDC** £4	— Proof *FDC**..........£2
— Proof *FDC** £2	1977 .... £0.50	1981 Proof *FDC**..........£4
1972 Proof *FDC** £4	— Proof *FDC** £2	
1973 Proof *FDC** £4	1978 .... £0.50	
	— Proof *FDC** £2	

4234 Five pence. 'New' omitted. As illustration

1982*........................ £2	1983* £2	1984*...........................£2
— Proof *FDC** £4	— Proof *FDC** £4	— Proof *FDC**..........£4

Obverse portrait by Raphael Maklouf

4371   4372

4371 Five pence. R. Crowned thistle

1985*.......................... £2	1988 ....£1	1990*............................£2
— Proof *FDC** £4	— Proof *FDC** £2	— Proof *FDC**..........£2
1986*.............................£2	1989 ....£1	— Proof in silver *FDC** £12
— Proof *FDC** £4	— Proof *FDC** £2	
1987.............................. £1		
— Proof *FDC** £2		

4372 Five pence. R. Crowned thistle: reduced diameter of 18mm

1990...............................£1	1992 ....£1	— Proof *FDC**..........£2
— Proof *FDC**..........£2	— Proof *FDC** £2	1996...............................£1
— Proof in silver *FDC** £10	1993* £2	— Proof *FDC**..............£2
— Proof piedfort in silver	— Proof *FDC**..............£4	— Proof in silver *FDC** £15
FDC (Issued:20,000)£20	1994 ....£1	1997...............................£1
1991...............................£1	— Proof *FDC** £2	— Proof *FDC**..........£2
— Proof *FDC**..........£2	1995 ....£1	

Obverse portrait by Ian Rank-Broadley

4670   4671

4670 Five pence. R. Crowned thistle

1998 .... £1
— Proof *FDC* * £3
1999 .... £1
— Proof *FDC* * £3
2000 .... £1
— Proof *FDC* * £3
— Proof in silver FDC (see PSS08)*£12
2001 .... £1
— Proof *FDC* * £3
2002 .... £1
— Proof *FDC* * £3
— Proof in gold *FDC* (see PGJS1) £225
2003 .... £1
— Proof *FDC* * £3

2004 .... £1
— Proof *FDC* * £3
2005 .... £1
— Proof *FDC* * £3
2006 .... £1
— Proof *FDC* * £3
— Proof in silver *FDC* (see PSS22)* £12
2007 .... £1
— Proof *FDC* * £3
2008 .... £1
— Proof *FDC* * £3
— Proof in silver *FDC* (see PSS27)* £12
— Proof in gold *FDC* (see PGEBCS)* £225
— Proof in platinum *FDC*
(see PPEBCS)* £325

4671 Five pence. R. A section of Our Royal Arms showing elements of all four quarterings accompanied by the words 'FIVE PENCE'(Reverse design: Matthew Dent)

2008 ....£3
— Proof *FDC* (in 2008 set, see PS96)* £3
— Proof in silver *FDC* (in 2008 set, see PSS28)* £12
— Proof piedfort in silver *FDC* (in 2008 set, see PSS29)* £25
— Proof in gold *FDC* (in 2008 set, see PGRSAS)* £225
— Proof in platinum *FDC* (in 2008 set, see PPRSAS)*............................£325
2009 ....£1
— Proof *FDC* (in 2009 set, see PS97)* £3
— Proof in silver *FDC* (in 2009 set, see PSS 37 ....£12
2010 ....£1
— Proof *FDC* (in 2010 set, see PS101)* £3
— Proof in silver *FDC* (in 2010 set, Edition: 3,500 see PSS41)* £12
2011 ....£3
— Proof *FDC* (in 2011 set, see PS104) * £3
— Proof in silver *FDC* (in 2011 set, Edition: 2,500, see PSS44) * £12

NICKEL PLATED STEEL

4672 Five pence.

2012 ....£3
— Proof *FDC* (in 2012 set, see PS107) * £5
— Proof in silver *FDC* (Edition: 995, see PSS47) * £30
— Proof in silver with selected gold plating *FDC* (Edition: 2,012, see PSS48) *......£30
— Proof in gold *FDC* (Edition: 150 see PGDJS)* £225

* *Coins marked thus were originally issued in Royal Mint sets.*

2013.. £3
—   Proof *FDC* (in 2013 set, see PS109) * £5
—   Proof in silver *FDC* (Edition: 2,013, see PSS50)* £30
—   Proof in gold *FDC* (Edition: 60 see PGCAS)* £225
2014
—   Proof *FDC* (in 2014 set, see PS112) * £5
—   Proof in silver *FDC* (Edition: 2,014 see PSS56)*

Obverse portrait by Arnold Machin

4231   4232

4231 Ten new pence. R. Lion passant guardant being royally crowned, being part of the crest of
England, and the inscription 'Ten New Pence' (Reverse design: Christopher Ironside)

1968..................... £0.50	1974 .... £0.50	1978 Proof *FDC**..........£4
1969.....................£0.50	— Proof *FDC** £3	1979..........................£0.50
1970.....................£0.50	1975 ....£0.50	— Proof *FDC*............ £3
1971.....................£0.50	— Proof *FDC** £3	1980..............................£1
— Proof *FDC** £3	1976 ....£0.50	— Proof *FDC**...........£3
1972 Proof *FDC** £4	— Proof *FDC** £3	1981..............................£1
1973.......................0.40	1977 ....0.50	— Proof *FDC**...........£3
— Proof *FDC** £3	— Proof *FDC** £3	

4232 Ten pence. 'New' omitted. As illustration

1982*................ £3	1983* £3	1984*..............................£3
— Proof *FDC** £4	— Proof *FDC** £4	— Proof *FDC**............£4

Obverse portrait by Raphael Maklouf

4366

4366 Ten pence. R. Lion passant guardant

1985*........................ £3	1988* £3	1991*.............................£4
— Proof *FDC* *.......£4	— Proof *FDC** £4	— Proof *FDC**...........£4
1986*........................£3	1989* £4	1992*.............................£3
— Proof *FDC**........£4	— Proof *FDC** £4	— Proof *FDC**...........£4
1987*........................£3	1990*.............................£4	— Proof in silver *FDC** £14
— Proof *FDC** £4	— Proof *FDC** £4	

* Coins marked thus were originally issued in Royal Mint sets.

4367 4650 4651

4367 Ten pence R Lion passant guardant: reduced diameter of 24.5mm

1992	£1	1995	£1
— Proof *FDC**	£3	— Proof *FDC**	£3
— Proof in silver *FDC** £10		1996	£1
— Proof piedfort in silver *FDC** (Issued: 14,167)£30		— Proof *FDC**	£3
1993*	£3	— Proof in silver *FDC**	£15
— Proof *FDC**	£4	1997	£1
1994*	£3	— Proof *FDC**	£3
— Proof *FDC**	£4		

Obverse portrait by Ian Rank-Broadley

4650 Ten pence. R. Lion passant guardant. (Illus. as 4232)

1998*	£3	2004	£1
— Proof *FDC**	£4	— Proof *FDC**	£3
1999*	£3	2005	£1
— Proof *FDC**	£4	— Proof *FDC**	£3
2000	£1	2006	£1
— Proof *FDC**	£3	— Proof *FDC**	£3
— Proof in silver FDC (see PSS08)*	£15	— Proof in silver *FDC* (see PSS22)*	£15
2001	£1	2007	£1
— Proof *FDC**	£3	— Proof *FDC*	£3
2002	£1	2008	£1
— Proof *FDC**	£3	— Proof *FDC**	£3
— Proof in gold *FDC* (see PGJS1)*	£500	— Proof in silver *FDC* (see PSS27)*	£15
2003	£1	— Proof in gold *FDC* (see PGEBCS)*	£400
— Proof *FDC**	£3	— Proof in platinum *FDC* (see PPEBCS)*	£650

4651 Ten pence. R. A section of Our Royal Arms showing elements of the first quartering accompanied by the words 'TEN PENCE'(Reverse design: Matthew Dent)

2008	£3
— Proof *FDC* (in 2008 set, see PS96)*	£6
— Proof in silver *FDC* (in 2008 set, see PSS28)*	£15
— Proof piedfort in silver *FDC* (in 2008 set, see PSS29)*	£25
— Proof in gold *FDC* (in 2008 set, see PGRSAS)*	£400
— Proof in platinum *FDC* (in 2008 set, see PPRSAS)*	£650
2009	£3
— Proof *FDC* (in 2009 set, see PS97)*	£6
— Proof in silver *FDC* (in 2009 set, see PSS 37)*	£15
2010	£3
— Proof *FDC* (in 2010 set, see PS101)*	£6
— Proof in silver *FDC* (in 2010 set, Edition: 3,500 see PSS 41)*	£15
2011	£3
— Proof *FDC* (in 2011 set, see PS104) *	£3
— Proof in silver *FDC* (in 2011 set, Edition: 2,500, see PSS44) *	£15

NICKEL PLATED STEEL

4652 Ten pence.
2012 .... £3
—   Proof *FDC* (in 2012 set, see PS107)* £3
—   Proof in silver *FDC* (Edition: 995, see PSS47)* £30
—   Proof in silver with selected gold plating *FDC* (Edition: 2,012, see PSS48)* £30
—   Proof in gold *FDC* (Edition: 150 see PGDJS)* £450
2013 .... £3
—   Proof FDC (in 2013 set, see PS109)* £5
—   Proof in silver FDC (Edition: 2,013, see PSS50)* £30
—   Proof in gold FDC (Edition: 60 see PGCAS)* £450

2014

—   Proof *FDC* (in 2014 set, see PS112)* £5

—   Proof in silver *FDC* (Edition: 2,014 see PSS56)*

CUPRO-NICKEL

Obverse portrait by Arnold Machin

4230

4230 Twenty pence. R. The Royal Badge of the Rose of England represented as a double rose
barbed and seeded, slipped and leaved and ensigned by a Royal Crown and the date of the
year with the inscription 'TWENTY PENCE' and the figure '20' superimposed on the stem
of the rose.(Reverse design: William Gardner)
1982 .... £0.50
—   Proof *FDC** £3
—   Proof piedfort in silver *FDC* (Issued: 10,000) £30
1983 .... £0.50
1984 .... £0.50
—   Proof *FDC** £3

Obverse portrait by Raphael Maklouf

4361

4361 Twenty pence. R. Crowned double rose

1985 .... £1   1990 .... £1   1995 .... £1
—   Proof *FDC** .... £3   —   Proof *FDC** .... £3   —   Proof *FDC** £3

* Coins marked thus were originally issued in Royal Mint sets.

1986*............................£3	1991 ....£1	1996.................................£1
— Proof *FDC** £4	— Proof *FDC** £3	— Proof *FDC** £3
1987 ....£1	1992.................................£1	— Proof in silver *FDC** £18
— Proof *FDC** £3	— Proof *FDC** £3	1997.................................£1
1988 ....£1	1993 ....£1	— Proof *FDC** £3
— Proof *FDC** £3	— Proof *FDC** £3	
1989 ....£1	1994 ....£1	
— Proof *FDC** £3	— Proof *FDC** £3	

Obverse portrait by Ian Rank-Broadley

4635

4635 Twenty pence. R. Crowned double rose.

1998......................................£1	2004 ....£1
— Proof *FDC** £3	— Proof *FDC** £3
1999......................................£1	2005 ....£1
— Proof *FDC** £3	— Proof *FDC** £3
2000......................................£1	2006 ....£1
— Proof *FDC** £3	— Proof *FDC** £3
— Proof in silver *FDC* (see PSS08) *£20	— Proof in silver *FDC* (see PSS22)* £20
2001 ....£1	2007 ....£1
— Proof *FDC** £3	— Proof *FDC** £3
2002......................................£1	2008 ....£1
— Proof *FDC** £3	— Proof *FDC** £3
— Proof in gold *FDC* (see PGJS1)*£450	— Proof in silver *FDC* (see PSS27)* £20
2003......................................£1	— Proof in gold *FDC* (see PGEBCS)* £350
— Proof *FDC** £3	— Proof in platinum *FDC* (see PPEBCS)* £550

4636

4636 Twenty pence. R. A section of Our Royal Arms showing elements of the second and forth quartering accompanied by the words 'TWENTY PENCE'(Reverse design: Matthew Dent)

2008...£3
— Proof *FDC* (in 2008 set, see PS96)*...£3
— Proof in silver *FDC* (in 2008 set, see PSS28)*.......................................£20
— Proof piedfort in silver *FDC* (in 2008 set, see PSS29)* £40
— Proof in gold *FDC* (in 2008 set, see PGRSAS)* £350
— Proof in platinum *FDC* (in 2008 set, see PPRSAS)*...............................£550

* Coins marked thus were originally issued in Royal Mint sets.

2009..£3
—   Proof *FDC* (in 2009 set, see PS97)*...£6
—   Proof in silver *FDC* (in 2009 set, see PSS 37)*....................................£20
2010..£3
—   Proof *FDC* (in 2010 set, see PS101)*...£6
—   Proof in silver *FDC* (in 2010 set, Edition: 3,500 see PSS 41)*..............£20
2011..£3
—   Proof *FDC* (in 2011 set, see PS104) *..£3
—   Proof in silver *FDC* (in 2011 set, Edition: 2,500, see PSS44) *...............£15

2012..£3
—   Proof *FDC* (in 2012 set, see PS107)*...£3
—   Proof in silver *FDC* (Edition: 995, see PSS47)*.....................................£30
—   Proof in silver with selected gold plating *FDC* (Edition: 2,012, see PSS48)*.......£30
—   Proof in gold *FDC* (Edition: 150 see PGDJS)* £350
2013..£3
—   Proof *FDC* (in 2013 set, see PS109)*...£5
—   Proof in silver *FDC* (Edition: 2,013, see PSS50)* £30
—   Proof in gold *FDC* (Edition: 60 see PGCAS)* £350
2014
—   Proof *FDC* (in 2014 set, see PS112)*...£5
—   Proof in silver *FDC* (Edition: 2,014 see PSS56)*

4636A — Error obverse – known as a Mule. The new reverse design by Matthew Dent does
not include the year date and this should have appeared on the obverse. A number of coins
were struck using the undated obverse die that had previously been used with the dated
reverse of the crowned double rose. (See Illus. 4635) £100

Obverse portrait by Arnold Machin

4223

4223 Fifty new pence (seven-sided). R. A figure of Britannia seated beside a lion, with a shield
resting against her right side, holding a trident in her right hand and an olive branch in her
left hand; and the inscription '50 NEW PENCE'. (Reverse design: Christopher Ironside)

1969............................. £3	1976 ....£2	1979...............................£2
1970............................. £4	— Proof *FDC** £3	— Proof *FDC** £3
1971 Proof *FDC** £5	1977 ....£2	1980...............................£2
1972 Proof *FDC** £5	— Proof *FDC** £3	— Proof *FDC** £3
1974 Proof *FDC** £5	1978 ....£2	1981...............................£2
1975 Proof *FDC** £5	— Proof *FDC** £3	— Proof *FDC** £3

* Coins marked thus were originally issued in Royal Mint sets.

4224   4225

4224 Accession to European Economic Community. R. The inscription 'FIFTY PENCE' and the date of the year, surrounded by nine hands, symbolizing the nine members of the community, clasping one another in a mutual gesture of trust, assistance and friendship. (Reverse design: David Wynne)

1973...£3
— Proof *FDC* ** £6

4224A —Design as 4224 above, but struck in very small numbers in silver on thicker blank. Sometimes referred to as a piedfort but not twice the weight of the regular cupro-nickel currency issue. The pieces were presented to EEC Finance Ministers and possibly senior officials on the occasion of the United Kingdom joining the European Economic Community..£2500

4225 **Fifty pence.** 'New' omitted. As illustration

1982......................£3   1983 ....£2   1984*...........................£3
— Proof *FDC** ....£3   — Proof *FDC* ....£3   — Proof *FDC* £3

Obverse portrait by Raphael Maklouf

4351

4351 **Fifty pence.** R. Britannia

1985...........................£3   1990* ....£4   1996*.............................£3
— Proof *FDC* ....£3   — Proof *FDC* ....£5   — Proof *FDC* £4
1986*..............................£3   1991*...................................£4   — Proof in silver *FDC* £20
— Proof *FDC* ....£3   — Proof *FDC* ....£5   1997..............................£2
1987*..........................£3   1992* ....£4   — Proof *FDC* £4
— Proof *FDC* ....£3   — Proof *FDC*..................£5   — Proof in silver *FDC*£20
1988*..........................£3   1993* £4
— Proof *FDC* ....£4   — Proof *FDC* £4
1989*..........................£4   1995* £3
— Proof *FDC* ....£3   — Proof *FDC* £4

* *Coins marked thus were originally issued in Royal Mint sets*
** *Issued as an individual proof coin and in the year set*

4352

4352 **Fifty pence** Presidency of the Council of European Community Ministers and completion of the Single Market. R A representation of a table on which are placed twelve stars, linked by a network of lines to each other and also to twelve chairs, around the table, on one of which appear the letters 'UK', and with the dates '1992' and '1993' above and the value '50 PENCE' below. (Reverse design: Mary Milner Dickens)

1992-1993 ....£12
— Proof *FDC** £12
— Proof in silver *FDC** (Issued: 26,890 ....£28
— Proof piedfort in silver *FDC* (Issued: 10,993) £60
— Proof in gold *FDC* (Issued: 1,864) £800

4353

4353 **Fifty pence** 50th Anniversary of the Normandy Landings on D-Day. R: A design representing the Allied invasion force of the D-Day landings heading for Normandy and filling the sea and sky, Together with the value '50 PENCE' (Reverse design: John Mills)

1994...£3
— Specimen in presentation folder...£5
— Proof *FDC**..£5
— Proof in silver *FDC* (Issued: 40,000) £35
— Proof piedfort in silver *FDC* (Issued: 10,000) £60
— Proof in gold *FDC* (Issued: 1,877)..£800

4354 **Fifty pence** R. Britannia: reduced diameter of 27.3mm

1997..£2
— Proof *FDC** £4
— Proof in silver *FDC* (Issued: 1,632) £25
— Proof piedfort in silver *FDC* (Issued: 7,192) £40

* *Coins marked thus were originally issued in Royal Mint sets*

Obverse portrait by Ian Rank-Broadley

4610

4610 Fifty pence. R. Britannia. (Illus. as 4351)

1998 .... £3	2006 .... £3
— Proof *FDC** £3	— Proof *FDC** £3
1999 .... £3	— Proof in silver *FDC* (see PSS22)* £25
2000 .... £3	2007 .... £3
— Proof *FDC** £3	— Proof *FDC** £3
2000 .... £3	2008 .... £3
— Proof *FDC** £3	— Proof *FDC** £3
— Proof in silver *FDC* (see PSS08)*£25	— Proof in silver *FDC* (see PSS27)* £30
2001 .... £3	— Proof in gold *FDC* (see PGEBCS)* £475
— Proof *FDC** £3	— Proof in platinum *FDC* (see PPEBCS)* £550
2002 .... £3	2009
— Proof *FDC** £3	— Proof *FDC* (in 2009 set, see PS100)* £15
— Proof in gold *FDC* (see PGJS1)* £450	— Proof in silver *FDC* (in 2009 set,
2003 ....£3	see PSS40)* £30
— Proof *FDC** £3	— Proof in gold *FDC* (in 2009 set,
2004 ....£3	see PG50PCS)* £475
— Proof *FDC** £3	— Proof piedfort in gold *FDC*
2005 £3	(see PG50PPCS)* £1200
— Proof *FDC** £3	

4611

4611 Fifty pence. R. Celebratory pattern of twelve stars reflecting the European flag with the dates 1973 and 1998 commemorating the 25th Anniversary of the United Kingdom's membership of the European Union and Presidency of the Council of Ministers. (Reverse design: John Mills)

1998..£2	
— Proof *FDC**...£5	
— Proof in silver *FDC* (Issued: 8,859)...£30	
— Proof piedfort in silver *FDC* (Issued: 8,440) £60	
— Proof in gold *FDC* (Issued: 1,177)...£450	
2009	
— Proof *FDC* (in 2009 set, see PS100)* £15	
— Proof in silver *FDC* (in 2009 set, see PSS40)*..£30	
— Proof in gold *FDC* (in 2009 set, see PG50PCS)* £450	
— Proof piedfort in gold *FDC* (see PG50PPCS) *...£1200	

* Coins marked thus were originally issued in Royal Mint sets.

           4612   4613

4612 Fifty pence. R. A pair of hands set against a pattern of radiating lines with the words
       'FIFTIETH ANNIVERSARY' and the value '50 PENCE' accompanied by the initials
       'NHS' which appear five times on the outer border. (Reverse design: David Cornell)
       1998 ....£2
       —   Specimen in presentation folder £3
       —   Proof in silver *FDC* (Issued: 9,032) £30
       —   Proof piedfort in silver *FDC* (Issued: 5,117) £60
       —   Proof in gold *FDC* (Issued: 651) £450
       2009
       —   Proof *FDC* (in 2009 set, see PS100)* £15
       —   Proof in silver *FDC* (in 2009 set, see PSS40)* £30
       —   Proof in gold *FDC* (in 2009 set, see PG50PCS)* £450
       —   Proof piedfort in gold *FDC* (see PG50PPCS) * £1200
4613 Fifty pence. Library commemorative. R. The turning pages of a book above the dates
       '1850 – 2000'and the value '50 PENCE', all above a classical library building on which
       the words 'PUBLIC LIBRARY' and, within the pediment , representations of compact
       discs. (Reverse design: Mary Milner Dickens)
       2000 ....£2
       —   Specimen in presentation folder £5
       —   Proof *FDC** £5
       —   Proof in silver *FDC* (Issued: 7,634) £28
       —   Proof piedfort in silver *FDC* (Issued: 5,721) £60
       —   Proof in gold *FDC* (Issued: 710) £450
       2009
       —   Proof *FDC* (in 2009 set, see PS100)* £15
       —   Proof in silver *FDC* (in 2009 set, see PSS40)* £30
       —   Proof in gold *FDC* (in 2009 set, see PG50PCS)* £450
       —   Proof piedfort in gold *FDC* (see PG50PPCS) * £1200

* Coins marked thus were originally issued in Royal Mint sets.

| 4614 | 4615 | 4616 |

4614 Fifty pence. Anniversary of the Suffragette Movement commemorative. R. The figure of
a suffragette chained to railings and holding a banner on which appear the letters 'WSPU',
to the right a ballot paper marked with a cross and the words 'GIVE WOMEN THE
VOTE', to the left the value '50 PENCE' and below and to the far right the dates '1903'
and '2003'. (Reverse design: Mary Milner Dickens)

2003..£2
— Specimen in presentation folder (Issued: 9,582)..£5
— Proof *FDC* (in 2003 set, see PS78)*...£5
— Proof in silver *FDC* (Issued: 6,267) £28
— Proof piedfort in silver *FDC* (Issued 6,795) £60
— Proof in gold *FDC* (Issued: 942)..£450
2009
— Proof *FDC* (in 2009 set, see PS100)*...£15
— Proof in silver *FDC* (in 2009 set, see PSS40)*..£30
— Proof in gold *FDC* (in 2009 set, see PG50PCS)* £450
— Proof piedfort in gold *FDC* (see PG50PPCS) *...£1200

4615 Fifty pence. 50th anniversary of the first sub four-minute mile. R. The legs of a running
athlete with a stylised stopwatch in the background and, below, the value '50 PENCE'.
(Reverse design: James Butler)

2004..£2
— Specimen in presentation folder (Issued: 10,371)...£5
— Proof *FDC* (in 2004 set, see PS81)*...£5
— Proof in silver *FDC* (Issued: 4,924)...£28
— Proof piedfort in silver *FDC* (Issued: 4,054) £60
— Proof in gold *FDC* (Issued: 644)..£450
2009
— Proof *FDC* (in 2009 set, see PS100)*...£15
— Proof in silver *FDC* (in 2009 set, seePSS40)*..£30
— Proof in gold *FDC* (in 2009 set, see PG50PCS)* £450
— Proof piedfort in gold *FDC* (see PG50PPCS)*... £1200

4616 Fifty pence. 250th anniversary of the publication of Samuel Johnson's Dictionary of the English
Language. R. Entries from Samuel Johnson's Dictionary of the English Language for the
words 'FIFTY' and 'PENCE', with the figure '50' above, and the inscription 'JOHNSON'S
DICTIONARY 1755' below. (Reverse design: Tom Phillips)

2005..£2
— Proof *FDC* (in 2005 set, see PS84)*...£5
— Proof in silver *FDC* (Issued: 4,029)...£28
— Proof piedfort in silver *FDC* (Issued: 3,808) £60
— Proof in gold *FDC* (Issued: 584)..£450
2009
— Proof *FDC* (in 2009 set, see PS100)*...£15
— Proof in silver *FDC* (in 2009 set, see PSS40)*..£30
— Proof in gold *FDC* (in 2009 set, see PG50PCS)* £450
— Proof piedfort in gold *FDC* (see PG50PPCS)*..£1200

* Coins marked thus were originally issued in Royal Mint sets.

18   DECIMAL COINAGE

4617   4618   4619

4617 Fifty pence. 150th anniversary of the institution of the Victoria Cross. R. A depiction of the obverse and reverse of a Victoria Cross with the date '29. JAN 1856' in the centre of the reverse of the Cross, the letters 'VC' to the right and the value 'FIFTY PENCE'. (Reverse design: Claire Aldridge)
2006...£2
—   Specimen in presentation folder with 4618...£7
—   Proof *FDC* (in 2006 set, see PS87)*...£5
—   Proof in silver *FDC* (Issued: 6,310)...£30
—   Proof piedfort in silver *FDC* (Issued: 3,532) (see PSS27)...................£60
—   Proof in gold *FDC* (Issued: 866)...£450
2009
—   Proof *FDC* (in 2009 set, see PS100)*...£15
—   Proof in silver *FDC* (in 2009 set, see PSS40)*......................................£30
—   Proof in gold *FDC* (in 2009 set, see PG50PCS)*....................................£450
—   Proof piedfort in gold *FDC* (see PG50PPCS)*..£1200

4618 Fifty pence. 150th anniversary of the institution of the Victoria Cross. R. A Depiction of a soldier carrying a wounded comrade with an outline of the Victoria Cross surrounded by a sunburst effect in the background and the value 'FIFTY PENCE'. (Reverse design: Clive Duncan)
2006...£2
—   Specimen in presentation folder with 4617...£7
—   Proof *FDC* (in 2006 set, see PS87)*...£5
—   Proof in silver *FDC* (Issued: 6,872)...£30
—   Proof piedfort in silver *FDC* (Issued: 3,415) (see PSS27)...................£60
—   Proof in gold *FDC* (Issued: 804)...£450
2009
—   Proof *FDC* (in 2009 set, see PS100)*...£15
—   Proof in silver *FDC* (in 2009 set, see PSS40)*......................................£30
—   Proof in gold *FDC* (in 2009 set, see PG50PCS)*....................................£450
—   Proof piedfort in gold *FDC* (see PG50PPCS)*..£1200

4619 Fifty pence. Centenary of the Founding of the Scouting Movement. R. A Fleur-de-lis superimposed over a globe and surrounded by the inscription 'BE PREPARED', and the dates '1907' and '2007' and the denomination 'FIFTY PENCE' (Reverse design: Kerry Jones)
2007...£2
—   Specimen in presentation folder...£7
—   Proof *FDC** (in 2007 set, see PS90)...£5
—   Proof in silver *FDC* (Issued: 10,895)...£30
—   Proof piedfort in silver *FDC** (Issued: 1,555)..£60
—   Proof in gold *FDC* (Issued: 1,250)...£450
2009
—   Proof *FDC* (in 2009 set, see PS100)*...£15
—   Proof in silver *FDC* (in 2009 set, see PSS40)*......................................£30
—   Proof in gold *FDC* (in 2009 set, see PG50PCS)*....................................£450
—   Proof piedfort in gold *FDC* (see PG50PPCS)*..£1200

Coins marked thus were originally issued in Royal Mint sets.

4620   4621

4620 Fifty pence. R. A section of Our Royal Arms showing elements of the third and fourth quarterings accompanied by the words 'FIFTY PENCE' (Reverse design: Matthew Dent)

2008 ....£3
— Proof *FDC* (in 2008 set, see PS96)* £5
— Proof in silver *FDC* (in 2008 set, see PSS28)* £30
— Proof piedfort in silver *FDC* (in 2008 set, see PSS29)* £60
— Proof in gold *FDC* (in 2008 set, see PGRSAS)* £450
— Proof in platinum *FDC* (in 2008 set, see PPRSAS)* £650

2009 ....£3
— Proof *FDC* (in 2009 set, see PS97)* £5
— Proof in silver *FDC* (in 2009 set, see PSS37)* £30
— Proof in gold *FDC* (in 2009 set, see PG50PCS)* £450
— Proof piedfort in gold *FDC* (see PG50PPCS)* £1200

2010..£3
— Proof *FDC* (in 2010 set, see PS101)* £5
— Proof in silver *FDC* (in 2010 set, Edition: 3,500, see PSS41)* £30

2011 ....£3
— Proof *FDC* (in 2010 set, see PS104)* £3
— Proof in silver *FDC* (in 2011 set, Edition: 2,500, see PSS44) * £15

2012 ....£3
— Proof *FDC* (in 2012 set, see PS107)* £3
— Proof in silver *FDC* (Edition: 995, see PSS47)* £30
— Proof in silver with selected gold plating *FDC* (Edition: 2,012, see PSS48) £30
— Proof in gold *FDC* (Edition: 150 see PGDJS)* £450

2013 ....£3
— Proof *FDC* (in 2013 set, see PS109) * £5
— Proof in silver *FDC* (Edition: 2,013, see PSS50)* £30
— Proof in gold *FDC* (Edition: 60 see PGCAS)* £475

2014
— Proof FDC (in 2014 set, see PS112)* £5
— Proof in silver FDC (Edition: 2,014 see PSS56)*

4621 Fifty pence. 250th Anniversary of the foundation of the Royal Botanical Gardens, Kew. R. A design showing the pagoda, a building associated with the Royal Botanical Gardens at Kew, encircled by a vine and accompanied by the dates '1759' and '2009', with the word 'KEW' at the base of the pagoda.(Reverse design: Christopher Le Brun)

2009 ....£3
— Specimen in presentation pack (Issued: 128,364)..£7
— Proof *FDC* (in 2009 set, see PS97)* £7
— Proof in silver *FDC* (Issued: 7,575) £30
— Proof piedfort in silver *FDC* (Issued: 2,967)) £55
— Proof in gold *FDC* (Issued: 629)...£450
— Proof piedfort in gold *FDC* (see PG50PPCS)* £1200

Coins marked thus were originally issued in Royal Mint sets.

4622 Fifty new pence. R. Britannia (See 4223).
2009
— Proof *FDC* (in 2009 set, see PS100)* £15
— Proof in silver *FDC* (in 2009 set, see PSS40)* £30
— Proof in gold *FDC* (in 2009 set, see PG50PCS)* £450
— Proof piedfort in gold *FDC* (in 2009 set, see PG50PPCS)* £1200

4623 Fifty new pence. Accession to European Economic Community R. Clasped hands.
(See 4224)

2009
— Proof *FDC* (in 2009 set, see PS100)* £15
— Proof in silver *FDC* (in 2009 set, see PSS40)* £30
— Proof in gold *FDC* (in 2009 set, see PG50PCS)* £450
— Proof piedfort in gold *FDC* (in 2009 set, see PG50PPCS)* £1200

4624 Fifty pence. R. Presidency of the Council of European Community Ministers and
completion of the Single Market. R. Conference table top and twelve stars. (See 4352)
2009
— Proof *FDC* (in 2009 set, see PS100)* £15
— Proof in silver *FDC* (in 2009 set, see PSS40)* £30
— Proof in gold *FDC* (in 2009 set, see PG50PCS)* £450
— Proof piedfort in gold *FDC* (in 2009 set, see PG50PPCS)* £1200

4625 Fifty pence. 50th Anniversary of the Normandy Landings on D-Day. R. Allied Invasion
Force (See 4353)
2009
— Proof *FDC* (in 2009 set, see PS100)* £15
— Proof in silver *FDC* (in 2009 set, see PSS40)* £30
— Proof in gold *FDC* (in 2009 set, see PG50PCS)* £450
— Proof piedfort in gold *FDC* (in 2009 set, see PG50PPCS)* £1200

4626

4626 Fifty pence. 100th Anniversary of Girl Guides. R. A design which depicts a repeating
pattern of the current identity of Girl Guiding, UK, accompanied by the inscription
'CELEBRATING ONE HUNDRED YEARS OF GIRLGUIDING UK' and the
denomination 'FIFTY PENCE' (Reverse design: Jonathan Evans and Donna Hainan)
2010 .... £1
— Specimen on presentation card (Issued: 99,075)) £5
— Specimen in presentation folder (Edition: 50,000) £7
— Proof *FDC* (in 2010 set, see PS101)* £7
— Proof in silver *FDC* (Issued: 5,271)) £30
— Proof piedfort in silver *FDC* (Issued: 2,879) £55
— Proof in gold *FDC* (Issued: 355) £525

4627   4628

4627 Fifty pence. Fifth Anniversary of the World Wildlife Fund. R. A design which features
50 different icons symbolising projects and programmes that the World   Wildlife
Fund has supported over the course of the last 50 years, with the Panda logo of the
organisation in the centre and the date '2011' below. (Reverse design: Matthew Dent)
2011 ....£1
— Specimen in presentation folder (Issued: 67,299) £7
— Proof *FDC* (in 2011 set, see PS104)..£7
— Proof in silver *FDC* (Issued: 24,870) £42
— Proof piedfort in silver *FDC* (Issued: 2,244,299)..£73
— Proof in gold *FDC* (Issued: 243) £725

4628 Fifty pence. R. A version of the Royal Arms with the inscription 'FIFTY PENCE' above
and the denomination '50' below. (Reverse design: Christopher Ironside).
2013
— Specimen in presentation folder £8
— Proof *FDC* (in 2013 set, see PS109)*...£5
— Proof silver *FDC* (Edition:4,500 including coins in sets) £45
— Proof piedfort in silver *FDC* (Edition: 3,513 including coins in sets) £90
— Proof in gold *FDC*(Edition: 450)...£800

4629

4629 Fifty pence. Centenary of the birth of Benjamin Britten. R. In the centre the name
'BENJAMIN BRITTEN' superimposed over musical staves with the inscription 'BLOW
BUGLE BLOW' above and 'SET THE WILD ECHOES FLYING' below. (Reverse
design: Tom Phillips).
2013
— Specimen in presentation folder £8
— Proof silver *FDC* (Edition: 2,000)..£45
— Proof piedfort in silver *FDC* (Edition: 1,000) £90
— Proof in gold *FDC*(Edition: 150)...£800

* Coins marked thus were originally issued in Royal Mint sets.

4630

4630 Fifty pence Commonwealth Games R. A design of a cyclist and a sprinter with the
Scottish Saltire bisecting the coin and the inscription 'XX COMMONWEALTH GAMES
GLASGOW' and the date'2014' (Reverse design: Alex Loudon with Dan Flashman).
2014
- Specimen in presentation folde...£10
- Proof *FDC* (in 2014 set, see PS112)*...£5
- Proof silver *FDC* (Edition: 4,500 including coins in sets) £45
- Proof piedfort in silver *FDC* (Edition: 3,513 including coins in sets) £90
- Proof in gold *FDC* (Edition: 450)...£800

NICKEL-BRASS
Obverse portrait by Arnold Machin

4221

4221 **One pound** R. The Ensigns Armorial of Our United Kingdom of Great Britain and
Northern Ireland with the value 'ONE POUND' below and the edge inscription
'DECUS ET TUTAMEN' (Reverse design: Eric Sewell)
1983 ....£5
- Specimen in presentation folder (Issued: 484,900) £5
- Proof *FDC* (in 1983 set, seePS33)* £5
- Proof in silver *FDC* (Issued: 50,000) £35
- Proof piedfort in silver *FDC* (Issued: 10,000) £125

4222

4222 **One pound** (Scottish design). R. A thistle eradicated enfiling a representation of Our
Royal Diadem with the value 'ONE POUND' below and the edge inscription 'NEMO
ME IMPUNE LACESSIT' (Reverse design: Leslie Durbin)
1984 ....£5
- Specimen in presentation folder (Issued: 27,960) £5
- Proof *FDC* (in 1984 set, see PS34)* £5
- Proof in silver *FDC* (Issued: 44,855) £30
- Proof piedfort in silver *FDC* (Issued: 15,000) £60

* Coins marked thus were originally issued in Royal Mint sets.

Obverse portrait by Raphael Maklouf

| 4331 | 4332 | 4333 |

4331 One pound (Welsh design). R. A leek eradicated enfiling a representation of Our Royal
Diadem with the value 'ONE POUND' below and the edge inscription 'PLEIDIOL
WYF I'M GWLAD". (Reverse design: Leslie Durbin)

1985 ....£4
— Specimen in presentation folder (Issued: 24,850) £4
— Proof *FDC* (in 1985 set, see PS35)* £5
— Proof in silver *FDC* (Issued: 50,000) £30
— Proof piedfort in silver *FDC* (Issued: 15,000) £60
1990 ....£5
— Proof *FDC* (in 1990 set, see PS45)* £6
— Proof in silver *FDC* (Issued: 23,277) £28

4332 One pound (Northern Irish design). R. A flax plant eradicated enfiling a representation
of Our Royal Diadem with value 'ONE POUND' below and the edge inscription
'DECUS ET TUTAMEN'. (Reverse design: Leslie Durbin)

1986 ....£5
— Specimen in presentation folder (Issued: 19,908) £5
— Proof *FDC* (in 1986 set, see PS37)* £4
— Proof in silver *FDC* (Issued: 37, 958) £30
— Proof piedfort in silver *FDC* (Issued: 15,000) £60
1991 ....£5
— Proof *FDC* (in 1991 set, see PS47)* £6
— Proof in silver *FDC* (Issued: 22,922) £28

4333 One pound (English design). R. An oak tree enfiling a representation of Our Royal
Diadem with the value 'ONE POUND' below and the edge inscription 'DECUS ET
TUTAMEN'. (Reverse design: Leslie Durbin)

1987 ....£4
— Specimen in presentation folder (Issued: 72,607) £4
— Proof *FDC* (in 1987 set, see PS39)* £6
— Proof in silver *FDC* (Issued: 50,000) £30
— Proof piedfort in silver *FDC* (Issued: 15,000) £60
1992 ....£5
— Proof *FDC* (in 1992 set, see PS49)* £6
— Proof in silver *FDC* (Issued: 13,065) £30

4334 One pound (Royal Shield). R. A Shield of Our Royal Arms ensigned by a representation
of Our Royal Crown with the value 'ONE POUND' below and the Edge inscription
'DECUS ET TUTAMEN'. (Reverse design: Derek Gorringe)

1988 ....£5
— Specimen in presentation folder (Issued: 29,550) £6
— Proof *FDC* (in 1988 set, see PS41)* £6
— Proof in silver *FDC* (Issued: 50,000) £35
— Proof piedfort in silver *FDC* (Issued: 10,000) £60

* Coins marked thus were originally issued in Royal Mint sets.

4335 **One pound** (Scottish design). Edge 'NEMO ME IMPUNE LACESSIT' (Illus. as 4222)
1989 ....£5
— Proof *FDC* (in 1989 set, see PS43)* £6
— Proof in silver *FDC* (Issued: 22,275) £30
— Proof piedfort in silver *FDC* (Issued: 10,000) £60
4336 **One pound** (Royal Arms design). Edge 'DECUS ET TUTAMEN' (Illus. as 4221)
1993 ....£5
— Proof *FDC* (in 1993 set, see PS51)* £6
— Proof in silver *FDC* (Issued: 16,526) £30
— Proof piedfort in silver *FDC* (Issued: 12,500) £60
4337 **One pound** (Scottish design). R: A Lion rampant within a double tressure flory counter-
flory, being that quartering of Our Royal Arms known heraldically as Scotland with
the value 'ONE POUND' below and the edge inscription 'NEMO ME IMPUNE
LACESSIT'. (Reverse design: Norman Sillman)
1994 ....£4
— Specimen in presentation folder £5
— Proof *FDC* (in 1994 set, see PS53)* £6
— Proof in silver *FDC* (Issued: 25,000) £30
— Proof piedfort in silver *FDC* (Issued: 11,722) £60
4338 **One pound** (Welsh design). R. A dragon passant, being Our badge for Wales with the
value 'ONE POUND' below and the edge inscription 'PLEIDIOL WYF I'M GWLAD'.
(Reverse design: Norman Sillman)
1995 ....£4
— Specimen in presentation folder, English version £5
— Specimen in presentation folder, Welsh version £10
— Proof *FDC* (in 1995 set, see PS55)* £5
— Proof in silver *FDC* (Issued: 27,445) £30
— Proof piedfort in silver *FDC* (Issued: 8,458) £70
4339 **One pound** (Northern Irish design). R. A Celtic cross charged at the centre with an
Annulet therein a Pimpernel flower and overall an ancient Torque, symbolizing that part
of Our Kingdom known as Northern Ireland with the value 'ONE POUND' below and
the edge inscription 'DECUS ET TUTAMEN'. (Reverse design: Norman Sillman)
1996 ....£4
— Specimen in presentation folder £6
— Proof *FDC* (in 1996 set, see PS57)* £6
— Proof in silver *FDC* (Issued: 25,000) £30
— Proof piedfort in silver *FDC* (Issued: 10,000 ....£60

4340

4340 **One pound** (English design) R. Three lions passant guardant, being that quartering of
Our Royal Arms known heraldically as *England*, with the value 'ONE POUND' below
and the edge inscription 'DECUS ET TUTAMEN.(Reverse design: Norman Sillman)
1997 ....£4
— Specimen in presentation folder (Issued 56,996) £5
— Proof *FDC* (in 1997 set, see PS59)* £5
— Proof in silver *FDC* (Issued: 20,137) £30
— Proof piedfort in silver *FDC* (Issued: 10,000) £60

* *Coins marked thus were originally issued in Royal Mint sets.*

Obverse portrait by Ian Rank-Broadley

4590

4590   One pound (Royal Arms design). Edge: 'DECUS ET TUTAMEN' (rev. as 4221)

    1998 ....£5
-   Proof *FDC* (in 1998 set, see PS61)* £6
-   Proof in silver *FDC* (Issued: 13,863) £30
-   Proof piedfort in silver *FDC* (Issued: 7,894) £60

    2003 ....£3
-   Specimen in presentation folder (Issued: 23,760)................................£5
-   Proof *FDC* (in 2003 set, see PS78)* £6
-   Proof in silver *FDC* (Issued: 15,830)...£30
-   Proof piedfort in silver *FDC* (Issued: 9,871) £60

    2008
-   Specimen in presentation folder (Issued: 18,336)................................£7
-   Proof *FDC* (in 2008 set, see PS93)* £6
-   Proof in silver *FDC* (Issued: 8,441) £30
-   Proof in gold *FDC* (Issued: 674)..£600
-   Proof in platinum *FDC* (in 2008 set, see PPEBCS)*......................£800

    2013. 30th Anniversary of the introduction of the £1 coin
-   Proof silver *FDC* (Edition: 3,500 in 3 coin sets, see PSS55)...........£60
-   Proof in gold *FDC* (Edition: 100 in 3 coin sets, see PG31S)..........£1000

4590A2008
-   Proof in silver with selected gold plating on reverse *FDC* (in 2008 set,
    see PSS30)*...£40

4591   One pound. (Scottish lion design). Edge: 'NEMO ME IMPUNE LACESSIT' (rev as 4337)

    1999 ....£3
-   Specimen in presentation folder...£5
-   Proof *FDC* (in 1999 set, see PS63)* £6
-   Proof in silver *FDC* (Issued: 16,328)...£30
-   Proof piedfort in silver *FDC* (Issued: 9,975) £60

    2008
-   Proof in gold *FDC* (in 2008 set, see PG1PCS)*................................£600

4591A1999
-   Proof in silver *FDC*, with reverse frosting, (Issued: 1,994)*...............£50

4591B2008
-   Proof in silver with selected gold plating on reverse *FDC* (in 2008 set, see PSS30)* £40

4592   One pound. (Welsh design). Edge: 'PLEIDIOL WYF I'M GWLAD' (rev. as 4338)

    2000...£3
-   Proof *FDC* (in 2000 set, see PS65)* £6
-   Proof in silver *FDC* (Issued: 15,913)...£30
-   Proof piedfort in silver *FDC* (Issued: 9,994) £60

    2008
-   Proof in gold *FDC* (in 2008 set, see PG1PCS)*................................£600

4592A2000
-   Proof in silver *FDC*, with reverse frosting, (Issued: 1,994)*...............£50

* Coins marked thus were originally issued in Royal Mint sets.

4592B2008
- Proof in silver with selected gold plating on reverse *FDC* (in 2008 set, see PSS30)* £40

4593 **One pound.** (Northern Irish design). Edge: 'DECUS ET TUTAMEN' (rev. as 4339)
2001 .... £3
- Proof *FDC* (in 2001 set, see PS68)* £6
- Proof in silver *FDC* (Issued: 11,697) £30
- Proof piedfort in silver *FDC* (Issued: 8,464) £60
2008
- Proof in gold *FDC* (in 2008 set, see PG1PCS)* £600

4593A2001
- Proof in silver *FDC*, with reverse frosting. (Issued: 1,540)* £60

4593B2008
- Proof in silver with selected gold plating on reverse *FDC* (in 2008 set, see PSS30)* £40

4594 **One pound.** (English design) Edge: 'DECUS ET TUTAMEN' (rev. as 4340)
2002 .... £3
- Proof *FDC* (in 2002 set, see PS72)* £6
- Proof in silver *FDC* (Issued: 17,693) £30
- Proof piedfort in silver *FDC* (Issued: 6,599) £60
- Proof in gold *FDC* (in 2002 set, see PGJS1)* £600
2008
- Proof in gold *FDC* (in 2008 set, see PG1PCS)* £600

4594A2002
- Proof in silver *FDC*, with reverse frosting, (Issued: 1,540)* £60

4594B2008
- Proof in silver with selected gold plating on reverse *FDC* (in 2008 set, see PSS30)* £40

4595

4595 **One pound.** Scotland R. A representation of the Forth Railway Bridge with a border of railway tracks and beneath, the value 'ONE POUND' and an incuse decorative feature on the edge symbolising bridges and pathways. (Reverse design: Edwina Ellis)
2004 .... £3
- Specimen in presentation folder (Issued: 24,014) £5
- Proof *FDC* (in 2004 set, see PS81)* £6
- Proof in silver *FDC* (Issued: 11,470) £30
- Proof piedfort in silver *FDC* (Issued: 7,013) £60
- Proof in gold *FDC* (Issued: 2,618) £600
2008
- Proof in gold *FDC* (in 2008 set, see PG1PCS)* £600

4595A One pound pattern. Scotland. R. Forth Railway Bridge but dated 2003 with plain edge and hallmark, reading "PATTERN" instead of "ONE POUND"
- Proof in silver *FDC** £25
- Proof in gold *FDC** £550

* *Coins marked thus were originally issued in Royal Mint sets.*

4595B   4596   4596B   4597

4595B **One pound pattern.** Scotland. R. Unicorn with the word "Pattern" below with plain
edge and hallmark and dated 2004. (Reverse design: Timothy Noad)
— Proof in silver *FDC** £25
— Proof in gold *FDC** £550

4595C
2008
— Proof in silver as 4595 with selected gold plating on reverse *FDC* (in 2008 set, see
PSS30)* £40

4596 **One pound.** Wales. R. A representation of the Menai Straits Bridge with a border of
railings and stanchions, the value 'ONE POUND' and an incuse decorative feature on the
edge symbolising bridges and pathways. (Reverse design: Edwina Ellis)
2005...£3
— Specimen in presentation folder (Issued: 24,802)...............................£6
— Proof *FDC* (in 2005 set, see PS84)* £6
— Proof in silver *FDC* (Issued: 8,371)...£35
— Proof piedfort in silver *FDC* (Issued: 6,007) £60
— Proof in gold *FDC* (Issued: 1,195)..£600
2008
— Proof in gold *FDC* (in 2008 set, see PG1PCS)* £600

4596A **One pound pattern.** Wales. R. Menai Straits Bridge but dated 2003 with plain edge and
hallmark
— Proof in silver *FDC* (in 2003 set, see PPS1)* £25
— Proof in gold *FDC* (in 2003 set, see PPS2)*.....................................£550

4596B **One pound pattern.** Wales. R Dragon and the word "Pattern" below with plain edge and
hallmark and dated 2004. (Reverse design: Timothy Noad)
— Proof in silver *FDC* (in 2004 set, see PPS3)* £25
— Proof in gold *FDC* (in 2004 set, see PPS4)*.....................................£550

4596C 2008
— Proof in silver as 4596 with selected gold plating on reverse *FDC* (in 2008 set,
see PSS30)*...£40

4597 **One pound.** Northern Ireland. R. A representation of the Egyptian Arch Railway Bridge
in County Down with a border of railway station canopy dags, the value 'ONE POUND'
and an incuse decorative feature on the edge symbolising bridges and pathways. (Reverse
design: Edwina Ellis)
2006...£4
— Specimen in presentation folder £6
— Proof *FDC* (in 2006 set, see PS87)* £8
— Proof in silver *FDC* (Edition: 20,000) £30
— Proof piedfort in silver *FDC* (Edition: 7,500)....................................£60
— Proof in gold *FDC* (Edition: 1,500) £600
2008
— Proof in gold *FDC* (in 2008 set, see PG1PCS)* £600

4597A **One pound pattern.** Northern Ireland. R. MacNeill's Egyptian Arch Railway Bridge but
dated 2003 with plain edge and hallmark
— Proof in silver *FDC* (in 2003 set, see PPS1)* £25
— Proof in gold *FDC* (in 2003 set, see PPS2)*.....................................£550

* Coins marked thus were originally issued in Royal Mint sets.

4597B   4598   4598A   4598B

4597B One pound pattern. Northern Ireland. R Stag and the word 'Pattern' below with plain
    edge and hallmark and dated 2004. (Reverse design: Timothy Noad)
    —   Proof in silver *FDC* (in 2004 set, see PPS3)*..£25
    —   Proof in gold *FDC* (in 2004 set, see PPS4)*..£550
4597C
    2008
    —   Proof in silver as 4597 with selected gold plating on reverse *FDC* (in 2008 set,
    see PSS30)*...£40
4598   **One pound. England.** R. A representation of the Gateshead Millennium Bridge with a
    border of struts, the value 'ONE POUND' and an incuse decorative feature on the edge
    symbolising bridges and pathways. (Reverse design: Edwina Ellis)
    2007..£4
    —   Specimen in presentation folder...£7
    —   Proof *FDC** (in 2007 set, see PS90)..£8
    —   Proof in silver *FDC* (Issued: 10,110)...£30
    —   Proof piedfort in silver *FDC* (Issued: 5,739)...£60
    —   Proof in gold *FDC* (Issued: 1,112)...£600
    2008
    —   Proof in gold *FDC* (in 2008 set, see PG1PCS)*...£600
4598A One pound pattern. England. R. Millennium Bridge but dated 2003 with plain edge and
    hallmark
    —   Proof in silver *FDC* (in 2003 set, see PSS1)*..£25
    —   Proof in gold *FDC* (in 2003 set, see PPS2)*...£550
4598B One pound pattern. England. R. Lion with the word 'Pattern' below with plain edge and
    hallmark and dated 2004. (Reverse design: Timothy Noad)
    —   Proof in silver *FDC* (in 2004 set, see PPS3)*..£25
    —   Proof in gold *FDC* (in 2004 set, see PPS4)*...£550
4598C 2008
    —   Proof in silver as 4598 with selected gold plating on reverse *FDC* (in 2008 set,
    see PSS30)*...£40
4599   **One pound.** (Scottish design). Edge 'NEMO ME IMPUNE LACESSIT' (rev. as 4222)
    2008
    —   Proof in gold *FDC* (in 2008 set, see PG1PCS)*...£600
4599A 2008
    —   Proof in silver with selected gold plating on reverse *FDC* (in 2008 set,
    see PSS30)*...£40
4600   **One pound.** (Welsh design). Edge 'PLEIDOL WYF I'M GWLAD' (rev. see 4331)
    2008
    —   Proof in gold *FDC* (in 2008 set, see PG1PCS)*...£600
4600A 2008
    —   Proof in silver with selected gold plating on reverse *FDC* (in 2008 set,
    see PSS30)*...£40
4601   **One pound.** (Northern Irish design). Edge 'DECUS ET TUTAMEN' (rev. see 4332)
    2008
    —   Proof in gold *FDC* (in 2008 set, see PG1PCS)*...£600

* *Coins marked thus were originally issued in Royal Mint sets.*

4601A2008
— Proof in silver with selected gold plating on reverse *FDC* (in 2008 set, see PSS30)* £40
4602 **One pound.** (English design). Edge 'DECUS ET TUTAMEN' (rev. see 4333)
2008
— Proof in gold *FDC* (in 2008 set, see PG1PCS)* £600
4602A2008
— Proof in silver with selected gold plating on reverse *FDC* (in 2008 set, see PSS30)* £40

4603 **One pound.** (Royal Shield). Edge 'DECUS ET TUTAMEN' (rev.as 4334).
2008
— Proof in gold FDC (in 2008 set, see PG1PCS)* £600
2013. 30th Anniversary of the introduction of the £1 coin.
— Proof silver FDC (Edition: 3,500 in 3 coin sets, see PSS55)* £60
— Proof in gold FDC (Edition: 100 in 3 coin sets, see PG31S)* £1000
4603A 2008
— Proof in silver with selected gold plating on reverse FDC (in 2008 set, see PSS30)* £40

4604

4604 **One pound.** R. A shield of Our Royal Arms with the words 'ONE' to the left and 'POUND' to the right and the edge inscription 'DECUS ET TUTAMEN' (Reverse design: Matthew Dent)
2008 ....£3
— Proof *FDC* (in 2008 set, see PS96)* £5
— Proof in silver *FDC* (Issued: 5,000) £30
— Proof piedfort in silver *FDC* (Edition: 8,000) £50
— Proof in gold *FDC* (Issued: 860)* £600
— Proof in platinum *FDC* (in 2008 set, see PPRSAS)* £800
2009 ....£3
— Specimen in presentation folder (Edition: 15,000) £7
— Proof *FDC* (in 2009 set, see PS97)* £5
— BU in silver (Edition: 50,000) £30
— Proof in silver *FDC* (Edition: 20,000 including coins in sets)..............£35
— Proof in gold *FDC* (Edition: 1,000) £600
2010 ....£3
— Proof *FDC* (in 2010 set, see PS101)* £5
— BU in silver (Edition: 50,000) £30
— Proof in silver *FDC* (Edition: 20,000 including coins in sets)..............£35
2011 ....£3
— Proof *FDC* (in 2011 set, see PS104) * £5
— BU in silver..£30
— Proof in silver *FDC* (in 2011 set, Edition: 2,500, see PSS44) * £35

* *Coins marked thus were originally issued in Royal Mint sets.*

2012 ....£3
  — Proof *FDC* (in 2012 set, see PS107)* £3
  — BU in silver £25
  — Proof in silver with selected gold plating *FDC* (Edition: 2,012, see PSS48) £40
  — Proof in gold *FDC* (Edition: 150 see PGDJS)* £600
2013 ....£3
  — Proof *FDC* (in 2013 set, see PS109) * £7
  — BU in silver £25
  — Proof in silver *FDC* (Edition: 10,000 including coins in sets)...............£40
  — Proof in gold *FDC* (Edition: 310 see PGCAS)* £1000
2014 ....£3
  — Proof *FDC* (in 2014 set, see PS112) *..£3
  — BU in silver £25
  — Proof in silver *FDC* (Edition: 2,014 see PSS56) *

4605   4606

4605 – One pound. London. R. A design which depicts the official badges of the capital
cities of the United Kingdom, with the badge of London being the principal focus,
accompanied by the name 'LONDON' and the denomination 'ONE POUND' with the
edge inscription 'DOMINE DIRIGE NOS'. (Reverse design: Stuart Devlin)
2010 ....£3
  — Specimen on presentation card (Issued: 66,313)....................................£5
  — Specimen in presentation folder with **4606** (Edition: 10,000) £14
  — Proof *FDC* (in 2010 set, see PS101)* £5
  — Proof in silver *FDC* (Issued: 7,693) £35
  — Proof piedfort in silver *FDC* (Issued: 3,682) £55
  — Proof in gold *FDC* (Issued: 950)..£600

4606 – One pound. Belfast. R. A design which depicts the official badges of the capital cities
of the United Kingdom, with the badge of Belfast being the principal focus, accompanied
by the name 'BELFAST' and the denomination 'ONE POUND' with the edge inscription
'PRO TANTO QUID RETRIBUAMUS' (Reverse design: Stuart Devlin)
2010 ....£3
  — Specimen on presentation card (Issued: 64,461)....................................£5
  — Specimen in presentation folder with **4605** (Edition: 10,000) £14
  — Proof *FDC* (in 2010 set, see PS101)* £5
  — Proof in silver *FDC* (Issued: 5,805) £35
  — Proof piedfort in silver *FDC* (Issued: 3,503) £55
  — Proof in gold *FDC* (Issued: 585)..£600

* Coins marked thus were originally issued in Royal Mint sets.

4607   4608

4607 **One pound. Edinburgh.** R. A design which depicts the official badges of the capital
cities of the United Kingdom, with the badge of Edinburgh being the principal focus,
accompanied by the name 'EDINBURGH' and the denomination 'ONE POUND' with
the edge inscription 'NISI DOMINUS'. (Reverse design: Stuart Devlin)

2011 ....£3
— Specimen in presentation folder with **4608** (Edition: 10,000) £14
— Proof *FDC* (in 2011 set, see PS104)* £8
— Proof in silver *FDC* (Issued: 4,973) £45
— Proof piedfort in silver *FDC* (Issued: 2,696)..£78
— Proof in gold *FDC* (Issued: 499) £950

4608 **One pound. Cardiff.** R. A design which depicts the official badges of the capital cities
of the United Kingdom, with the badge of Cardiff being the principal focus, accompanied
by the name 'CARDIFF' and the denomination 'ONE POUND' with the edge inscription
'Y DDRAIG GOCH DDYRY CYCHWYN ' (Reverse design: Stuart Devlin)

2011 ....£3
— Specimen in presentation folder with **4607** (Edition: 10,000)...............£14
— Proof *FDC* (in 2011 set, see PS104) * £8
— Proof in silver *FDC* (Issued: 5,553) £45
— Proof piedfort in silver *FDC* (Issued: 1,615)..£78
— Proof in gold *FDC* (Issued: 524) £950

4720   4721

4720 **One pound. England.** R. Depicts an oak branch paired with a Tudor-inspired rose
with the denomination 'ONE POUND' below and the edge inscription 'DECUS ET
TUTAMEN'. (Reverse design: Timothy Noad)

2013 ....£3
— Specimen in presentation folder with **4721** £18
— Proof *FDC* (in 2013 set, see PS109) * £7
— Proof in silver *FDC* (Edition: 9,513including coins in sets) £50
— Proof piedfort in silver *FDC* (Edition: 5,013 including coins in sets) £100
— Proof in gold *FDC* (Edition: 560 including coins in sets)...................£1000

4721 **One pound. Wales.** R. Depicts a leek and a daffodil with their leaves entwined and the
denomination 'ONE POUND' below and the edge inscription 'PLEIDIOL WYF I'M
GWLAD'. (Reverse design: Timothy Noad)

2013 ....£3
— Specimen in presentation folder with **4720** £18
— Proof FDC (in 2013 set, see PS109) * £7
— Proof in silver FDC (Edition: 9,513 including coins in sets) £50
— Proof piedfort in silver FDC (Edition: 5,013 including coins in sets)..................£100
— Proof in gold FDC (Edition: 560 including coins in sets) £1000

* *Coins marked thus were originally issued in Royal Mint sets.*

4722   4723

4722 One pound. Northern Ireland. R. Depicts a flax and shamrock being the principle
focus for Northern Ireland accompanied by the denomination 'ONE POUND' and
the edge inscription 'DECUS ET TUTANEM. (Reverse design: Timothy Noad)
2014 ....£3
—   Specimen in presentation folder with 4723 ....£18
—   Proof *FDC* (in 2014 set, see PS112) * £7
—   Proof in silver *FDC* (Edition: 6,028 including coins in sets) £50
—   Proof piedfort in silver *FDC* (Edition: 3,014 including coins in sets) £100
—   Proof in gold *FDC* (Edition: 560 including coins in sets) £1000

4723 One pound. Scotland. R. Depicts the thistle and bluebell being the principle focus for
Scotland accompanied by the denomination 'ONE POUND' and the edge inscription
'NEMO ME IMPUNE LACESSIT'. (Reverse design: Timothy Noad)
2014 ....£3
—   Specimen in presentation folder with 4722 ....£18
—   Proof *FDC* (in 2014 set, see PS112)* £7
—   Proof in silver *FDC* (Edition: 6,028 including coins in sets) £50
—   Proof piedfort in silver *FDC* (Edition: 3,014 including coins in sets) £100
—   Proof in gold *FDC* (Edition: 560 including coins in sets) £1000

NICKEL-BRASS

Obverse portrait by Raphael Maklouf

4311

4311 Two pounds. R. St. Andrew's cross with a crown of laurel leaves and surmounted by a
thistle of Scotland with date '1986' above. Edge 'XIII COMMONWEALTH GAMES
SCOTLAND' (Reverse design: Norman Sillman)
1986...£5
—   Specimen in presentation folder £8
—   Proof *FDC** £10
—   500 silver (Issued: 58,881) £18
—   Proof in silver *FDC* (Issued: 59,779) £35
—   Proof in gold *FDC* (Issued: 3,277)...£525

* Coins marked thus were originally issued in Royal Mint sets.

4312   4313   4314

4312 **Two pounds** 300th Anniversary of Bill of Rights. R Cypher of W&M (King William and Queen Mary) interlaced surmounting a horizontal Parliamentary mace and a representation of the Royal Crown above and the dates '1689'and '1989' below, all within the inscription 'TERCENTENARY OF THE BILL OF RIGHTS'. (Reverse design: John Lobban)

1989 ....£5
— Specimen in presentation folder £8
— Proof *FDC* (in 1989 set, see PS43)* £10
— Proof in silver *FDC* (Issued: 25,000) £35
— Proof piedfort in silver *FDC* (in 1989 set, seePSS01)* £60

4313 **Two pounds** 300th Anniversary of Claim of Right (Scotland). R. As 4312, but with Crown of Scotland and the inscription 'TERCENTENARY OF THE CLAIM OF RIGHT'. (Reverse design: John Lobban)

1989 ....£15
— Specimen in presentation folder £20
— Proof *FDC* (in 1989 set, see PS43)* £15
— Proof in silver *FDC* (Issued: 24,852) £35
— Proof piedfort in silver *FDC* (in 1989 set, seePSS01)* £60

4314 **Two pounds** 300th Anniversary of the Bank of England. R: Bank's original Corporate Seal, with Crown & Cyphers of William III & Mary II and the dates '1694' and '1994'. Edge 'SIC VOS NON VOBIS'on the silver and base metal versions. (Reverse design: Leslie Durbin)

1994 ....£5
— Specimen in presentation folder £8
— Proof *FDC* (in 1994 set, see PS53)* £10
— Proof in silver *FDC* (Issued: 27, 957) £35
— Proof piedfort in silver *FDC* (Issued: 9,569) £60
— Proof in gold *FDC* (Issued: 1,000) £550

4314A— Gold Error – known as a Mule coin. £2500

The obverse of the 1994 Bank of England issue should have included the denomination 'TWO POUNDS' as this was not included in the design of the commemorative reverse. An unknown number of coins were struck and issued in gold using the die that was reserved for the Double Sovereign or Two Pound coins in the sovereign series. The Royal Mint wrote to its retail customers inviting them to return the error coin for replacement with the correct design. No details are known as to how many were returned, nor how many exist in the market. The incorrect obverse can be seen at **4251** in the section listing Gold Sovereigns; the correct obverse is at **4311**.

* Coins marked thus were originally issued in Royal Mint sets.

4315   4316

4315 **Two pounds** 50th Anniversary of the End of World War II. R: A stylised representation of a
dove as the symbol of Peace. Edge '1945 IN PEACE GOODWILL 1995'. (Reverse design:
John Mills)

1995 .... £5
— Specimen in presentation folder £8
— Proof *FDC* (in 1995 set, see PS55)* £10
— Proof in silver *FDC* (Issued: 35,751) £35
— Proof piedfort in silver *FDC* (Edition: 10,000) £60
— Proof in gold *FDC* (Issued: 2,500) £525

4316 **Two pounds** 50th Anniversary of the Establishment of the United Nations. R: 50th
Anniversary symbol and a fanning pattern of flags with the inscription 'NATIONS UNITED
FOR PEACE' above and the dates '1945-1995' below. (Reverse design: Michael Rizzello)

1995 .... £5
— Specimen in presentation folder £7
— Specimen in card (issued as part of multi country United Nations Collection) £7
— Proof in silver *FDC* (Edition: 175,000) £35
— Proof piedfort in silver *FDC* (Edition: 10,000) £60
— Proof in gold *FDC* (Edition: 17,500) £525

4317

4317 **Two pounds** European Football Championships. R: A stylised representation of a football
with the date '1996' centrally placed and surrounded by sixteen small rings. Edge:
'TENTH EUROPEAN CHAMPIONSHIP'. (Reverse design: John Mills)

1996 .... £6
— Specimen in presentation folder £8
— Proof *FDC* (in 1996 set, see PS57)* £10
— Proof in silver *FDC* (Issued: 25,163) £35
— Proof piedfort in silver *FDC* (Issued: 7,634) £60
— Proof in gold *FDC* (Issued: 2,098) £525

4317A Incorrect blank. When struck the coins have a dished appearance on both the obverse
and reverse but several pieces in gold have been reported where the surface of the coins
is flat. Enquiries at the Mint are continuing with a view to understanding how this could
have occurred £1500

* *Coins marked thus were originally issued in Royal Mint sets.*

Bimetallic issues

4318

4318 Two pounds Bimetallic currency issue. R. Four concentric circles representing the Iron
Age, 18th Century industrial development, silicon chip, and Internet. Edge: 'STANDING
ON THE SHOULDERS OF GIANTS'. (Reverse design: Bruce Rushin)

1997..£5
— Specimen in presentation folder...£8
— Proof *FDC* (in 1997 set, see PS59)* £10
— Proof in silver FDC (Issued: 29,910) £32
— Proof piedfort in silver *FDC* (Issued: 10,000) £60
— Proof in gold *FDC* (Issued: 2,482)..£525

Obverse portrait by Ian Rank-Broadley

4570

4570 Two pounds. Bimetallic currency issue. R. Four concentric circles, representing the Iron
Age, 18th Century industrial development, silicon chip and Internet. Edge: 'STANDING
ON THE SHOULDERS OF GIANTS'. (Rev. as 4318)

1998..£5
— Proof *FDC* (in 1998 set, see PS61)* £10
— Proof in silver *FDC* (Issued: 19,978)..£32
— Proof piedfort in silver *FDC* (Issued: 7,646) £60
1999..£4
2000..£4
— Proof *FDC* (in 2000 set, see PS65)* £10
— Proof in silver *FDC* (in 2000 set, see PSS10)* £35
2001..£4
— Proof *FDC* (see PS68)* £10
2002..£4
— Proof *FDC* (in 2002 set, see PS72)* £10
— Proof in gold *FDC* (in 2002 set, see PGJS1)* £525
2003..£4
— Proof *FDC* (see PS78)* £10
2004..£4
— Proof *FDC* (in 2004 set, see PS81)* £10
2005..£4
— Proof *FDC* (see PS84)* £10
2006..£4
— Proof *FDC* (in 2006 set, see PS87)* £10
— Proof in silver *FDC* (in 2006 set, see PSS22)* £35

* Coins marked thus were originally issued in Royal Mint sets.

2007..£4
2008..£4
—   Proof *FDC* (in 2008 set, see PS93)*..£10
2009..£4
—   Proof *FDC* (in 2009 set, see PS97)..£10
—   Proof in silver *FDC* (in 2009 set, see PSS37)*...£35
2010..£4
—   Proof *FDC* (in 2010 set, see PS101)*...£10
—   Proof in silver *FDC* (in 2010 set, see PSS41)*...£35
2011..£4
—   Proof *FDC* (in 2010 set, see PS104)*...£10
—   Proof in silver *FDC* (in 2010 set, see PSS44)*...£35
2012..£4
—   Proof *FDC* (in 2012 set, see PS107)*..£3
—   Proof in silver *FDC* (Edition: 2,012, see PSS47)*..£30
—   Proof in gold *FDC* (Edition: 150 see PGDJS)*...£800
2013..£4
—   Proof FDC (in 2013 set, see PS109)*..£5
—   Proof in silver FDC (Edition: 2,013, see PSS50)*..£30
—   Proof in gold FDC (Edition: 50 see PGCAS)*...£1000
2014..£4
—   Proof FDC (in 2014 set, see PS112)*..£5
—   Proof in silver FDC (Edition: 2,014 see PSS56)*
4571   Two pounds. Rugby World Cup. R. In the centre a rugby ball and goal posts surrounded
by a stylised stadium with the denomination 'TWO POUNDS' and the date '1999'. Edge:
'RUGBY WORLD CUP 1999'. (Reverse design: Ron Dutton)
1999..£5
—   Specimen in presentation folder...£8
—   Proof *FDC* (in 1999 set, see PS63)*...£10
—   Proof in silver *FDC* (Issued: 9,665)...£40
—   Proof in gold *FDC* (Issued: 311)...£550

4571A   4572

4571A— Proof piedfort in silver with coloured hologram on reverse *FDC* (Issued: 10,000) ..£150
4572   Two pounds. Marconi commemorative. R. Decorative radio waves emanating from a spark
of electricity linking the zeros of the date to represent the generation of the signal that crossed
the Atlantic with the date '2001' and the denomination 'TWO POUNDS'. Edge: 'WIRELESS
BRIDGES THE ATLANTIC MARCONI 1901'. (Reverse design: Robert Evans)
2001..£5
—   Specimen in presentation folder...£7
—   Proof *FDC* (in 2001 set, see PS68)*...£10
—   Proof in silver *FDC* (Issued: 11,488)..£35
—   Proof piedfort in silver *FDC* (Issued: 6,759)..£60
—   Proof in gold *FDC* (Issued: 1,658)..£525
4572A— Proof in silver *FDC*, with reverse frosting. (Issued: 4,803 in a 2-coin set with a
Canadian $5 Marconi silver proof)...£60

* Coins marked thus were originally issued in Royal Mint sets.

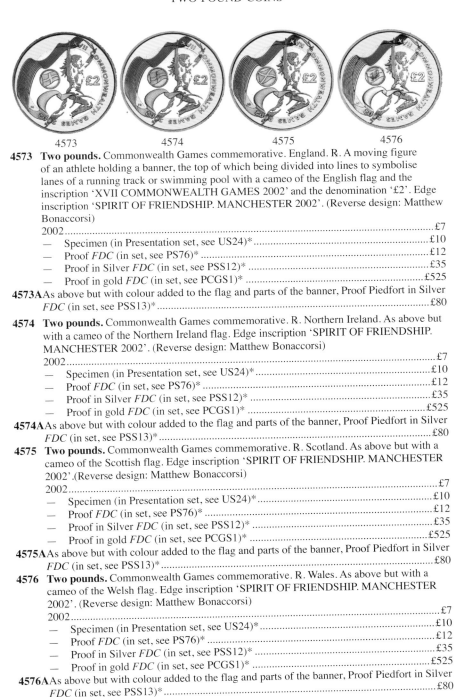

| 4573 | 4574 | 4575 | 4576 |

4573 **Two pounds.** Commonwealth Games commemorative. England. R. A moving figure of an athlete holding a banner, the top of which being divided into lines to symbolise lanes of a running track or swimming pool with a cameo of the English flag and the inscription 'XVII COMMONWEALTH GAMES 2002' and the denomination '£2'. Edge inscription 'SPIRIT OF FRIENDSHIP. MANCHESTER 2002'. (Reverse design: Matthew Bonaccorsi)

2002...£7
 — Specimen (in Presentation set, see US24)*..£10
 — Proof *FDC* (in set, see PS76)* £12
 — Proof in Silver *FDC* (in set, see PSS12)* £35
 — Proof in gold *FDC* (in set, see PCGS1)* £525

4573A As above but with colour added to the flag and parts of the banner, Proof Piedfort in Silver
 FDC (in set, see PSS13)* £80

4574 **Two pounds.** Commonwealth Games commemorative. R. Northern Ireland. As above but with a cameo of the Northern Ireland flag. Edge inscription 'SPIRIT OF FRIENDSHIP. MANCHESTER 2002'. (Reverse design: Matthew Bonaccorsi)

2002...£7
 — Specimen (in Presentation set, see US24)*..£10
 — Proof *FDC* (in set, see PS76)* £12
 — Proof in Silver *FDC* (in set, see PSS12)* £35
 — Proof in gold *FDC* (in set, see PCGS1)* £525

4574A As above but with colour added to the flag and parts of the banner, Proof Piedfort in Silver
 FDC (in set, see PSS13)* £80

4575 **Two pounds.** Commonwealth Games commemorative. R. Scotland. As above but with a cameo of the Scottish flag. Edge inscription 'SPIRIT OF FRIENDSHIP. MANCHESTER 2002'.(Reverse design: Matthew Bonaccorsi)

2002...£7
 — Specimen (in Presentation set, see US24)*..£10
 — Proof *FDC* (in set, see PS76)* £12
 — Proof in Silver *FDC* (in set, see PSS12)* £35
 — Proof in gold *FDC* (in set, see PCGS1)* £525

4575A As above but with colour added to the flag and parts of the banner, Proof Piedfort in Silver
 FDC (in set, see PSS13)* £80

4576 **Two pounds.** Commonwealth Games commemorative. R. Wales. As above but with a cameo of the Welsh flag. Edge inscription 'SPIRIT OF FRIENDSHIP. MANCHESTER 2002'. (Reverse design: Matthew Bonaccorsi)

2002...£7
 — Specimen (in Presentation set, see US24)*..£10
 — Proof *FDC* (in set, see PS76)* £12
 — Proof in Silver *FDC* (in set, see PSS12)* £35
 — Proof in gold *FDC* (in set, see PCGS1)* £525

4576A As above but with colour added to the flag and parts of the banner, Proof Piedfort in Silver
 FDC (in set, see PSS13)* £80

* Coins marked thus were originally issued in Royal Mint sets.

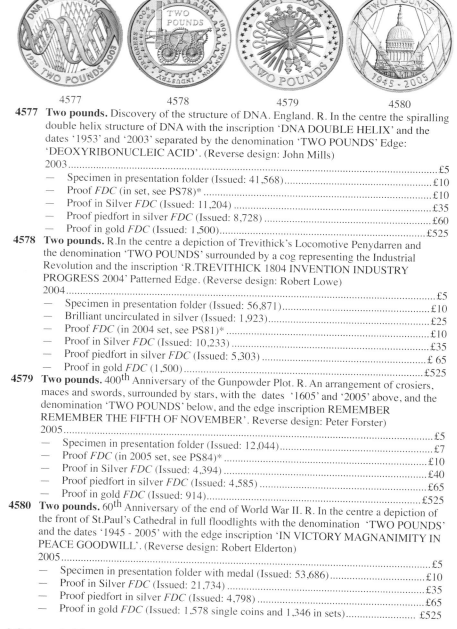

| 4577 | 4578 | 4579 | 4580 |

4577 **Two pounds.** Discovery of the structure of DNA. England. R. In the centre the spiralling double helix structure of DNA with the inscription 'DNA DOUBLE HELIX' and the dates '1953' and '2003' separated by the denomination 'TWO POUNDS' Edge: 'DEOXYRIBONUCLEIC ACID'. (Reverse design: John Mills) 2003......£5

— Specimen in presentation folder (Issued: 41,568).............£10
— Proof *FDC* (in set, see PS78)*......£10
— Proof in Silver *FDC* (Issued: 11,204) £35
— Proof piedfort in silver *FDC* (Issued: 8,728) £60
— Proof in gold *FDC* (Issued: 1,500)......£525

4578 **Two pounds.** R.In the centre a depiction of Trevithick's Locomotive Penydarren and the denomination 'TWO POUNDS' surrounded by a cog representing the Industrial Revolution and the inscription 'R.TREVITHICK 1804 INVENTION INDUSTRY PROGRESS 2004' Patterned Edge. (Reverse design: Robert Lowe) 2004......£5

— Specimen in presentation folder (Issued: 56,871).............£10
— Brilliant uncirculated in silver (Issued: 1,923)......£25
— Proof *FDC* (in 2004 set, see PS81)*......£10
— Proof in Silver *FDC* (Issued: 10,233) £35
— Proof piedfort in silver *FDC* (Issued: 5,303) £65
— Proof in gold *FDC* (1,500)......£525

4579 **Two pounds.** 400th Anniversary of the Gunpowder Plot. R. An arrangement of crosiers, maces and swords, surrounded by stars, with the dates '1605' and '2005' above, and the denomination 'TWO POUNDS' below, and the edge inscription REMEMBER REMEMBER THE FIFTH OF NOVEMBER'. Reverse design: Peter Forster) 2005......£5

— Specimen in presentation folder (Issued: 12,044).............£7
— Proof *FDC* (in 2005 set, see PS84)*......£10
— Proof in Silver *FDC* (Issued: 4,394) £40
— Proof piedfort in silver *FDC* (Issued: 4,585) £65
— Proof in gold *FDC* (Issued: 914)......£525

4580 **Two pounds.** 60th Anniversary of the end of World War II. R. In the centre a depiction of the front of St.Paul's Cathedral in full floodlights with the denomination 'TWO POUNDS' and the dates '1945 - 2005' with the edge inscription 'IN VICTORY MAGNANIMITY IN PEACE GOODWILL'. (Reverse design: Robert Elderton) 2005......£5

— Specimen in presentation folder with medal (Issued: 53,686).............£10
— Proof in Silver *FDC* (Issued: 21,734) £35
— Proof piedfort in silver *FDC* (Issued: 4,798) £65
— Proof in gold *FDC* (Issued: 1,578 single coins and 1,346 in sets)...... £525

* Coins marked thus were originally issued in Royal Mint sets.

4581 4582 4583

4581 **Two pounds.** 200th Anniversary of the birth of Isambard Brunel. R. In the centre a portrait of the engineer with segments of a wheel and bridge in the background surrounded by links of a heavy chain and the date '2006' and the denomination 'TWO POUNDS', with the edge inscription '1806 - 1859 ISAMBARD KINGDOM BRUNEL ENGINEER'. (Reverse design: Rod Kelly)

2006...£5
— Specimen in presentation folder (with **4582**)..£10
— Proof *FDC* (in 2006 set, see PS87)*..£10
— Proof in silver *FDC* (Issued: 7,251)...£35
— Proof piedfort in silver *FDC* (Issued: 3,199) (see PSS25)* £65
— Proof in gold *FDC* (Issued: 1,071)...£525

4582 **Two pounds.** 200th Anniversary of the birth of Isambard Brunel. R. In the centre a section of the roof of Paddington Station with 'BRUNEL' below and the date '2006' and the denomination 'TWO POUNDS', with the edge inscription 'SO MANY IRONS IN THE FIRE'. (Reverse design: Robert Evans)

2006...£4
— Specimen in presentation folder (with **4581**)..£10
— Proof *FDC* (in 2006 set, see PS87)*..£10
— Proof in silver *FDC* (Issued: 5,375)...£35
— Proof piedfort in silver *FDC* (Issued: 3,018) (see PSS25)*...................................£65
— Proof in gold *FDC* (Issued: 746)...£525

4583 **Two pounds.** Tercentenary of the Act of Union between England and Scotland. R. A design dividing the coin into four quarters, with a rose and a thistle occupying two of the quarters, and a portcullis in each of the other two quarters. The whole is overlaid with a linking jigsaw motif and surrounded by the dates '1707' and '2007' and the denomination 'TWO POUNDS', with an edge inscription 'UNITED INTO ONE KINGDOM' (Reverse design : Yvonne Holton)

2007...£5
— Specimen in presentation folder..£8
— Proof *FDC* (in 2007 set, see PS90)*..£10
— Proof in Silver *FDC* (Issued: 8,310) £35
— Proof piedfort in silver *FDC* (Issued: 4,000) £60
— Proof in gold *FDC* (Issued: 750)..£700

4583A – Error edge. The obverse and reverse designs of the Act of Union silver proof combined with the edge inscription of the Abolition of Slave Trade issue (4584 below). The edge inscription is impressed on the blanks prior to the striking of the obverse and reverse designs and whilst one example has been reported, and confirmed as genuine by the Royal Mint, it seems possible that a small batch may have been produced and other pieces have yet to be detected. £1000

* Coins marked thus were originally issued in Royal Mint sets.

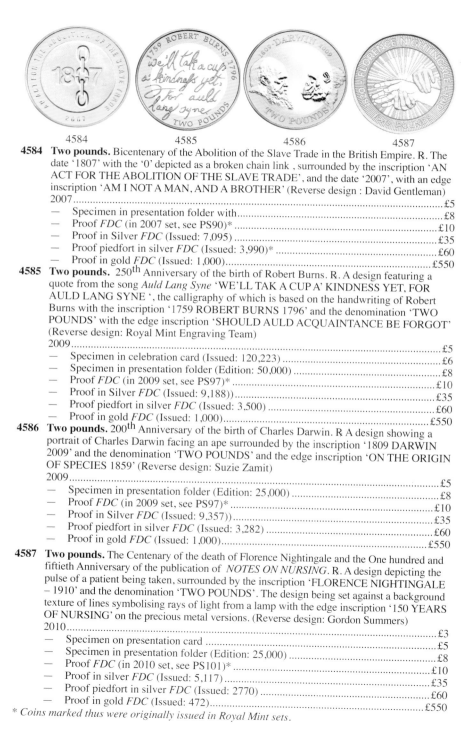

4584   4585   4586   4587

4584   **Two pounds.** Bicentenary of the Abolition of the Slave Trade in the British Empire. R. The date '1807' with the '0' depicted as a broken chain link , surrounded by the inscription 'AN ACT FOR THE ABOLITION OF THE SLAVE TRADE', and the date '2007', with an edge inscription 'AM I NOT A MAN, AND A BROTHER' (Reverse design : David Gentleman) 2007...£5
—   Specimen in presentation folder with..£8
—   Proof *FDC* (in 2007 set, see PS90)*...£10
—   Proof in Silver *FDC* (Issued: 7,095) £35
—   Proof piedfort in silver *FDC* (Issued: 3,990)* £60
—   Proof in gold *FDC* (Issued: 1,000)..£550

4585   **Two pounds.** 250th Anniversary of the birth of Robert Burns. R. A design featuring a quote from the song *Auld Lang Syne* 'WE'LL TAK A CUP A' KINDNESS YET, FOR AULD LANG SYNE ', the calligraphy of which is based on the handwriting of Robert Burns with the inscription '1759 ROBERT BURNS 1796' and the denomination 'TWO POUNDS' with the edge inscription 'SHOULD AULD ACQUAINTANCE BE FORGOT' (Reverse design: Royal Mint Engraving Team) 2009...£5
—   Specimen in celebration card (Issued: 120,223) £6
—   Specimen in presentation folder (Edition: 50,000) £8
—   Proof *FDC* (in 2009 set, see PS97)*...£10
—   Proof in Silver *FDC* (Issued: 9,188))...£35
—   Proof piedfort in silver *FDC* (Issued: 3,500) £60
—   Proof in gold *FDC* (Issued: 1,000)..£550

4586   **Two pounds.** 200th Anniversary of the birth of Charles Darwin. R A design showing a portrait of Charles Darwin facing an ape surrounded by the inscription '1809 DARWIN 2009' and the denomination 'TWO POUNDS' and the edge inscription 'ON THE ORIGIN OF SPECIES 1859' (Reverse design: Suzie Zamit) 2009...£5
—   Specimen in presentation folder (Edition: 25,000) £8
—   Proof *FDC* (in 2009 set, see PS97)*...£10
—   Proof in Silver *FDC* (Issued: 9,357))...£35
—   Proof piedfort in silver *FDC* (Issued: 3,282) £60
—   Proof in gold *FDC* (Issued: 1,000)..£550

4587   **Two pounds.** The Centenary of the death of Florence Nightingale and the One hundred and fiftieth Anniversary of the publication of *NOTES ON NURSING.* R. A design depicting the pulse of a patient being taken, surrounded by the inscription 'FLORENCE NIGHTINGALE – 1910' and the denomination 'TWO POUNDS'. The design being set against a background texture of lines symbolising rays of light from a lamp with the edge inscription '150 YEARS OF NURSING' on the precious metal versions. (Reverse design: Gordon Summers) 2010...£3
—   Specimen on presentation card £5
—   Specimen in presentation folder (Edition: 25,000) £8
—   Proof *FDC* (in 2010 set, see PS101)*...£10
—   Proof in silver *FDC* (Issued: 5,117)...£35
—   Proof piedfort in silver *FDC* (Issued: 2770) £60
—   Proof in gold *FDC* (Issued: 472)..£550

* Coins marked thus were originally issued in Royal Mint sets.

4588

4588 Two pounds. 500th Anniversary of the launch of the Mary Rose. R. A depiction of the ship based on a contemporary painting, surrounded by a cartouche bearing the inscription 'THE MARY ROSE' above, the denomination 'TWO POUNDS' below, and a rose to the left and right. The lettering on the reverse is rendered in the Lombardic style employed on the coins of Henry VII, and with the edge inscription 'YOUR NOBLEST SHIPPE 1511' (Reverse design: John Bergdahl)

2011 ....£3
—   Specimen in presentation folder (Edition: 20,000) £8
—   Proof *FDC* (in 2011 set, see PS104)* £10
—   Proof in silver *FDC* (Issued: 6,618)..£50
—   Proof piedfort in silver *FDC* (Issued: 2,394) £88
—   Proof in gold *FDC* (Issued: 692) £800

4589   4730

4589 Two pounds. The 400th Anniversary of the King James Bible. R. A design focusing on the opening verse of St John's Gospel, 'IN THE BEGINNING WAS THE WORD', showing the verse as printing blocks on the left and the printed page on the right, with the inscription' KING JAMES BIBLE' above and the dates '1611-2011'below with the edge inscription 'THE AUTHORISED VERSION'. (Reverse design: Paul Stafford and Benjamin Wright)

2011 ....£3
—   Specimen in presentation folder (Edition: 20,000) £8
—   Proof *FDC* (in 2011 set, see PS104)* £10
—   Proof in silver *FDC* (Issued: 4,494)..£50
—   Proof piedfort in silver *FDC* (Issued: 2,394) £88
—   Proof in gold *FDC* (Issued: 355) £800

4730 Two pounds. The 200th Anniversary of the birth of Charles Dickens. R. A silhouette profile of the writer through the titles of his works, greater prominence being given to those that are more well known, with the inscription 'CHARLES DICKENS 1870' to the left with the edge inscription 'SOMETHING WILL TURN UP' (Reverse design:)

2012 ....£3
—   Specimen in presentation folder (Edition: 20,000) £8
—   Proof *FDC* (in 2012 set, see PS107)* £10
—   Proof in silver *FDC* (Edition: 8,000 including coins in sets) £50
—   Proof piedfort in silver *FDC* (Edition: 2,000) £88
—   Proof in gold *FDC* (Edition: 1,000) £800

* Coins marked thus were originally issued in Royal Mint sets.

4731   4732   4733

4731 **Two pounds.** 350th Anniversary of the Guinea, R. A depiction of the Royal Arms based on that on the reverse of the 'SPADE GUINEA' of George III with and surrounded by the inscription 'ANNIVERSARY OF THE GOLDEN GUINEA' and the date '2013' below with the edge inscription 'WHAT IS A GUINEA ? 'TIS A SPENDID THING'. (Reverse design: Anthony Smith).

2013 ....£4
—   Specimen in presentation folder £10
—   Proof *FDC* (in 2013 set, see PS109)* £10
—   Proof in silver *FDC* (Edition: 12,500 including coins in sets) £50
—   Proof piedfort in silver *FDC* (Edition: 4,013 including coins in sets) £100
—   Proof in gold FDC (Edition: 1,110 including coins in sets) £900

4732 **Two pounds.** 150th Anniversary of the London Underground. R.The Roundel logo of the London underground system with the dates '1863' above and '2013' below and the edge inscription 'MIND THE GAP'. (Reverse design: Edwina Ellis).

2013 ....£4
—   Specimen in presentation folder with 4733..£20
—   Proof *FDC* (in 2013 set, see PS109)* £10
—   Proof in silver *FDC* (Edition: 12,500 including coins in sets) £50
—   Proof piedfort in silver *FDC* (Edition: 4,013 including coins in sets) £100
—   Proof in gold *FDC* (Edition: 960 including coins in sets)...............................£900

4733 **Two pounds.** 150th Anniversary of the London Underground. R. Depicts a train emerging from a tunnel with the date '1863' to the left and the inscription 'LONDON UNDERGROUND' and the date '2013' to the right with a patterned edge inspired by the map of the underground network. (Reverse design: Edward Barber and Jay Osgerby).

2013 ....£4
—   Specimen in presentation folder with 4732..£20
—   Proof *FDC* (in 2013 set, see PS109)* £10
—   Proof in silver *FDC* (Edition: 12,500 including coins in sets)..........................£50
—   Proof piedfort in silver *FDC* (Edition: 4,013 including coins in sets) £100
—   Proof in gold *FDC* (Edition: 960 including coins in sets)...............................£900

* Coins marked thus were originally issued in Royal Mint sets.

4734

4734 Two pounds. Trinity House R. A depiction of a lighthouse lens, surrounded by the inscription 'TRINITY HOUSE' and the dates '1514' and '2014' with the denomination 'TWO POUNDS' with the edge inscription 'SERVING THE MARINER' (Reverse design: Joe Whitlock Blundell with David Eccles).

2014 ....£4
— Specimen in presentation folder...£10
— Proof *FDC* (in 2014 set, see PS112)* £10
— Proof in silver *FDC* (Edition: 3,714 including coins in sets)...............................£50
— Proof piedfort in silver *FDC* (Edition: 3,514 including coins in sets) £100
— Proof in gold *FDC* (Edition: including coins in sets)..£900

4735

4735 Two pounds. World War I R. A depiction pf Lord Kitchener pointing, with the inscription 'YOUR COUNTRY NEEDS YOU' below the effigy of Lord Kitchener, and the inscription 'THE FIRST WORLD WAR 1914-1918' and the date '2014' with the edge inscription 'THE LAMPS ARE GOING OUT ALL OVER EUROPE' (Reverse design: John Bergdahl).

2014..£4
— Specimen in presentation folder...£10
— Proof *FDC* (in 2014 set, see PS112)* £10
— Proof in silver *FDC* (Edition: 8,014 including coins in sets) £50
— Proof piedfort in silver *FDC* (Edition: 4,514 including coins in sets)..................£100
— Proof in gold *FDC* (Edition: 825 including coins in sets) £750

For further £2 commemorative issues, see Olympic and Paralympic coins on pages 608-609.
* *Coins marked thus were originally issued in Royal Mint sets.*

CUPRO-NICKEL

Note for Collectors

The collecting of crown size coins is one of the most popular pursuits among new and established coin collectors. Before decimalisation in 1971, crowns had a nominal denomination of five shillings and this was then changed to twenty five pence in 1972 when the Silver Wedding commemorative was issued. Over time with increasing metal, manufacturing and distribution costs, the production of coins with such a low face value was not economic and the decision was taken to change to a higher value that would last for many years. The first of the five pound crowns was issued in 1990 to mark the ninetieth birthday of The Queen Mother. It seems sensible to group all of the crown size coins together and therefore the earlier twenty five pence issues are not listed between the twenty pence and fifty pence denominations but appear below.

Obverse portrait by Arnold Machin

4226

4226 **Twenty-five pence** (crown). Silver Wedding Commemorative R. The initials E P on a background of foliage, figure of Eros above the Royal Crown with the inscription 'ELIZABETH AND PHILIP'above and the dates '20 NOVEMBER 1947 – 1972' below.(Reverse design: Arnold Machin)

1972..£2
—   Proof *FDC* (in 1972 Set, See PS22)*..£6
—   Silver proof *FDC* (Issued: 100,000) £45

4227

4227 **Twenty-five pence** (crown). Silver Jubilee Commemorative R. The Ampulla and Anointing Spoon encircled by a floral border and above a Royal Crown. (Obverse and reverse design: Arnold Machin)

1977..£2
—   Specimen in presentation folder..£2
—   Proof *FDC* (in 1977 Set, See PS27)*..£5
—   Silver proof *FDC* (Issued: 377,000) £40

* Coins marked thus were originally issued in Royal Mint sets.

4228   4229

4228 Twenty-Five pence (crown). Queen Mother 80th Birthday Commemorative R. In the
centre a portrait of The Queen Mother surrounded by bows and lions with the inscription
'QUEEN ELIZABETH THE QUEEN MOTHER 4 AUGUST 1980' (Reverse design:
Richard Guyatt)

1980 ....£3
— Specimen in presentation folder...£5
— Silver proof *FDC* (Issued: 83,672) £45

4229 **Twenty-five pence.**(crown). Royal Wedding Commemorative R.Portrait of the Prince of Wales and Lady Diana Spencer with the inscription 'HRH THE PRINCE OF WALES AND LADY DIANA SPENCER 1981' (Reverse design: Philip Nathan)

1981 ....£3
—   Specimen in presentation folder..£5
—   Silver proof *FDC* (Issued: 218,142) £45

Obverse portrait by Raphael Maklouf

4301

4301 **Five pounds** (crown). Queen Mother's 90th birthday commemorative. R. A Cypher in the letter E in duplicate above a Royal Crown flanked by a rose and a thistle all within the inscription 'QUEEN ELIZABETH THE QUEEN MOTHER' and the dates '1900 – 1990' (Reverse design: Leslie Durbin)

1990 ....£10
—   Specimen in presentation folder (Issued: 45,250)...£12
—   Proof in silver *FDC* (Issued: 56,102)...£45
—   Proof in gold *FDC* (Issued: 2,500)..£1250

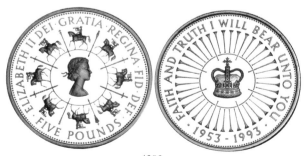

4302

4302 **Five pounds** (crown). 40th Anniversary of the Coronation. R. St Edward's Crown encircled by forty trumpets all within the inscription 'FAITH AND TRUTH I WILL BEAR UNTO YOU' and the dates '1953 – 1993'(Reverse design: Robert Elderton)

1993 ....£7
—   Specimen in presentation folder..£9
—   Proof *FDC* (in 1993 set, see PS51)* £12
—   Proof in silver *FDC* (Issued: 58,877)..£45
—   Proof in gold *FDC* (Issued: 2,500)...£1250

* Coins marked thus were originally issued in Royal Mint sets.

4303

4303 Five pounds (crown). 70th Birthday of Queen Elizabeth II. R. A representation of Windsor Castle with five flag poles, two holding forked pennants with anniversary dates '1926' and '1996', the other flags are Royal Arms, the Union flag and Our Personal flag. Edge inscription: 'VIVAT REGINA ELIZABETHA'. (Reverse design: Avril Vaughan)

1996 ....£10
— Specimen in presentation folder (issued: 73,311) £12
— Proof *FDC* (in 1996 set, See PS57)* £12
— Proof in silver *FDC* (Issued: 39,336) £50
— Proof in gold *FDC* (Issued: 2,127) £1250

4304

4304 Five pounds (crown). Golden Wedding of Queen Elizabeth II and Prince Philip. Conjoint portraits of The Queen and Prince Philip. R. A pair of shields, chevronwise, on the left, OurRoyal Arms, on the right, the shield of Prince Philip, above a Royal Crown separating the dates '1947' and '1997' with the date '20 NOVEMBER', below an anchor cabled with the denomination 'FIVE POUNDS'. (Obverse design: Philip Nathan, reverse design: Leslie Durbin)

1997 ....£7
— Specimen in presentation folder £10
— Proof *FDC* (in 1997 set, See PS59)* £15
— Proof in silver *FDC* (Issued: 33,689) £50
— Proof in gold *FDC* (Issued: 2,574) £1250

Coins marked thus were originally issued in Royal Mint sets.

Obverse portrait by Ian Rank-Broadley

4550

4550 Five pounds (crown). Prince Charles' 50th Birthday. R. A portrait of Prince Charles and in the background words relating to the work of The Prince's Trust. A circumscription of 'FIFIETH BIRTHDAY OF HRH PRINCE OF WALES' and below 'FIVE POUNDS' flanked by the anniversary dates '1948' and '1998'. (Reverse design: Michael Noakes / Robert Elderton)

1998 ....£7
  — Specimen in presentation folder £10
  — Proof *FDC* (in 1998 set, see PS 61)* £15
  — Proof in silver *FDC* (Issued: 13,379) £60
  — Proof in gold *FDC* (Issued: 773) £1250

4551

4551 Five pounds (crown). Diana, Princess of Wales Memorial. R. A portrait of Diana, Princess of Wales with the dates '1961' and '1997', and the circumscription 'IN MEMORY OF DIANA, PRINCESS OF WALES' with the value 'FIVE POUNDS' (Reverse design: David Cornell)

1999 ....£7
  — Specimen in presentation folder £12
  — Proof *FDC* (in 1999 set, see PS63)* £15
  — Proof in silver *FDC* (Issued: 49,545) £50
  — Proof in gold *FDC* (Issued: 7,500) £1250

* Coins marked thus were originally issued in Royal Mint sets.

4552	4552A

4552 Five pounds (crown). Millennium commemorative. R. A representation of the dial of a
clock with hands set at 12 o'clock with a map of the British Isles and the dates '1999' and
'2000' and the words 'ANNO DOMINI' and the value 'FIVE POUNDS'. Edge: 'WHAT'S
PAST IS PROLOGUE' in serif or sans serif font. (Reverse design: Jeffrey Matthews)

1999...£7
— Specimen in presentation folder...£10
— Proof in silver *FDC* (Issued: 49,057)...£50
— Proof in gold *FDC* (Issued: 2,500)...£1250
2000
— Specimen in presentation folder...£20
— Proof *FDC* (in 2000 set, see PS65)* £15
— Proof in gold *FDC* (Issued: 1,487)...£1250

4552A 2000
— Specimen in presentation folder with Dome mint mark £20
(See illustration above - the mintmark is located within the shaded area at 3 o'clock).

4552B 2000
— Proof in silver *FDC* (Issued: 14,255)...£60
(The reverse design is the same as the 1999 issue but with the British Isles highlighted with 22 ct. gold)

4553

4553 Five pounds (crown). Queen Mother commemorative. R. A portrait of the Queen Mother
flanked by groups of people with the circumscription 'QUEEN ELIZABETH THE QUEEN
MOTHER' the anniversary dates '1900' and '2000' below, and the denomination 'FIVE
POUNDS'. Below the portrait a representation of her signature. (Reverse design:
Ian Rank-Broadley)

2000...£7
— Specimen in presentation folder...£10
— Proof in silver *FDC* (Issued: 31,316)...£50
— Proof piedfort in silver *FDC* (Issued: 14,850) £80
— Proof in gold *FDC* (Issued: 3,000)...£1250

* Coins marked thus were originally issued in Royal Mint sets.

4554

4554 Five pounds (crown). Victorian anniversary. R. A classic portrait of the young Queen Victoria
      based on the Penny Black postage stamp with a V representing Victoria, and taking the form
      of railway lines and in the background the iron framework of the Crystal Palace, and the
      denomination '5 POUNDS' and the dates '1901' and '2001'. (Reverse design:
      Mary Milner-Dickens)
      2001...£7
      —   Specimen in presentation folder...£10
      —   Proof *FDC* (in 2001 set, see PS68)*...£15
      —   Proof in silver *FDC* (Issued: 19,216)...£55
      —   Proof in gold *FDC* (Issued: 2,098)...£1250
4554A— Proof in silver *FDC* with 'reverse frosting' giving matt appearance (Issued:596)
          (Crown issued with sovereigns of 1901 and 2001)*..£200
4554B— Proof in gold *FDC* with 'reverse frosting' giving matt appearance.(Issued:733)
          (Crown issued with four different type sovereigns of Queen Victoria, - Young
          Head with shield, and Young Head with St.George reverse, Jubilee Head and
          Old Head.)*..£1350

4555

4555 Five pounds (crown). Golden Jubilee commemorative 2002. O. New portrait of The Queen
      with the denomination 'FIVE POUNDS'. R. Equestrian portrait of The Queen with the
      inscription 'ELIZABETH II DEI GRA REGINA FID DEF' around the circumference and
      'AMOR POPULI PRAESIDIUM REG' within, and the date '2002' below separated by the
      central element of the Royal Arms. (Obverse and reverse designs: Ian Rank-Broadley)
      2002...£7
      —   Specimen in presentation folder...£10
      —   Proof *FDC* (in 2002 set, see PS 72)*..£15
      —   Proof in silver *FDC* (Issued: 54,012)..£55
      —   Proof in gold *FDC* (Issued: 3,500)..£1250

* *Coins marked thus were originally issued in Royal Mint sets.*

4556

4556 Five pounds (crown). Queen Mother Memorial 2002. ℞. Three quarter portrait of the
Queen Mother within a wreath with the inscription 'QUEEN ELIZABETH THE QUEEN
MOTHER' and the dates '1900' and '2002', with an edge inscription 'STRENGTH,
DIGNITY AND LAUGHTER'. (Reverse design: Avril Vaughan)

2002...£8
  — Specimen in presentation folder..£15
  — Proof in silver *FDC* (Issued: 16,117) £55
  — Proof in gold *FDC* (Issued: 2,086)...£1250

4557

4557 Five pounds (crown). Coronation commemorative 2003. O. Profile portrait of The Queen
in linear form facing right with the inscription 'ELIZABETH II DEI GRATIA REGINA
F D'. ℞. In the centre the inscription 'GOD SAVE THE QUEEN' surrounded by the
inscription 'CORONATION JUBILEE' the denomination 'FIVE POUNDS' and the date
'2003'. (Obverse and reverse designs: Tom Phillips)

2003...£8
  — Specimen in presentation folder (Issued: 100,481)..£10
  — Proof *FDC* (in 2003 set, see PS 78)* £15
  — Proof in silver *FDC* (Issued: 28,758)...£55
  — Proof in gold *FDC* (Issued: 1,896)...£1250

* Coins marked thus were originally issued in Royal Mint sets.

4558

4558 Five pounds (crown). Centenary of Entente Cordiale 2004. R. In the centre the head and shoulders of Britannia and her French counterpart Marianne with the inscription 'ENTENTE CORDIALE' separated by the dates '1904' and '2004'. Obv. as 4556. (Reverse design: David Gentleman)

2004..£8
— Specimen in presentation folder (Issued: 16,507)...£20
— Proof *FDC* with reverse frosting (Issued: 6,065)...£20
— Proof in silver *FDC* (Issued: 11,295) £60
— Proof Piedfort in silver *FDC* (Issued: 2,500) £150
— Proof in gold *FDC* (Issued: 926)...£1250
— Proof Piedfort in platinum *FDC* (Issued: 501)...£3600

4559

4559 Five pounds (crown). Two hundredth anniversary of the Battle of Trafalgar 2005. R. A depiction of the two British ships, HMS Victory and Temeraine, in the midst of the battle, the central design surrounded by the inscription 'TRAFALGAR' and the dates '1805' and '2005' with the edge inscription 'ENGLAND EXPECTS THAT EVERY MAN WILL DO HIS DUTY'. Obv. as 4556. (Reverse design: Clive Duncan)
Note: Only the precious metal versions have edge inscriptions, the CuNi coins have a milled edge.

2005..£9
— Specimen in presentation folder (Issued: 79,868)...£12
— Proof *FDC* (in 2005 set, see PS84)* £12
— Proof in silver *FDC* (Issued: 21,448) £55
— Proof piedfort in silver *FDC* (see PSS21)* £90
— Proof in gold *FDC* (Issued: 1,805)..£1250

* *Coins marked thus were originally issued in Royal Mint sets.*

4560

4560 **Five pounds** (crown). Two hundredth anniversary of the death of Nelson 2005. R. A portrait of Lord Nelson in the uniform of a Vice Admiral accompanied by the inscription 'HORATIO NELSON' and the dates '1805' and '2005' with the edge inscription 'ENGLAND EXPECTS THAT EVERY MAN WILL DO HIS DUTY'. Obv. as 4556. (Reverse design: James Butler)
Note: Only the precious metal versions have edge inscriptions, the CuNi coins have a milled edge.
2005..£10
— Specimen in presentation folder (Issued: 72,498)..£12
— Proof *FDC* (in 2005 set, see PS84)*...£12
— Proof in silver *FDC* (Issued: 12,852)..£60
— Proof piedfort in silver *FDC* (see PSS21)*..£90
— Proof in gold *FDC* (Issued: 1,760) £1250
— Proof piedfort in platinum *FDC* (Edition: 200) £3600

4561

4561 **Five pounds** (crown). 80th Birthday of Her Majesty Queen Elizabeth II. R. A fanfare of regal trumpets with the inscription 'VIVAT REGINA' and the dates '1926' and '2006', and the edge inscription 'DUTY SERVICE FAITH'. Obv. as 4556. (Reverse design: Danuta Solowiej-Wedderburn)
2006..£7
— Specimen in presentation folder...£10
— Proof *FDC* (in 2006 set, see PS87)*...£15
— Proof in silver *FDC* (Issued: 20,790)...£55
— Proof in gold *FDC* (Issued: 2,750)...£1250
— Proof piedfort in platinum *FDC* (Issued: 250)...£3600
4561A— Proof piedfort in silver with selected gold plating *FDC* (Issued: 5,000)..................£80

* *Coins marked thus were originally issued in Royal Mint sets.*

4562

4562 **Five pounds** (crown). Diamond Wedding Anniversary of Her Majesty Queen Elizabeth II and The Duke of Edinburgh. O. Conjoint portrait of The Queen and Prince Philip. R. The Rose window of Westminster Abbey with the inscription 'TVEATVR VNITA DEVS', the dates '1947' and '2007', the denomination 'FIVE POUNDS', and the edge inscription 'MY STRENGTH AND STAY' (Obverse design: Ian Rank-Broadley, reverse design: Emma Noble) 2007...£7

  — Specimen in presentation folder...£10
  — Proof *FDC* (in 2007 set, see PS90)*...£15
  — Proof in silver *FDC* (Issued: 15,186)..£55
  — Proof piedfort in silver *FDC* (Issued: 2,000) £80
  — Proof in gold *FDC* (Issued: 2,380)..£1250
  — Proof piedfort in platinum *FDC* (Issued: 250)...£3600

4563   4564

4563 **Five pounds** (crown). 450th Anniversary of the Accession of Queen Elizabeth I. R A portrait of Queen Elizabeth I surrounded by four Tudor roses placed at the centre points of connecting arches, with two side panels containing details taken from carvings made by Robert Dudley, Earl of Leicester, found at the Tower of London, the design being encircled by the inscription 'ELIZABETH REGINA' with the dates 'MDLVIII' and 'MMVIII' with the edge inscription 'I HAVE REIGNED WITH YOUR LOVES' on the precious metal versions. Obv. as 4556. (Reverse design: Rod Kelly). 2008..£7

  — Specimen in presentation folder (Issued: 26,700)...£10
  — Proof *FDC* (in 2008 set, see PS93)*...£15
  — Proof in silver *FDC* (Issued: 10,398)...£15
  — Proof piedfort in silver *FDC* (Edition: 5,000)...£60
  — Proof in gold *FDC* (Issued: 1,500)..£1250
  — Proof piedfort in platinum *FDC* (Issued: 150)...£3600

* Coins marked thus were originally issued in Royal Mint sets.

4564 **Five pounds** (crown). Prince of Wales 60th Birthday. R. A profile portrait of His Royal Highness The Prince of Wales with the inscription 'THE PRINCE OF WALES' above and '1948 ICH DIEN 2008' below with the edge inscription 'SIXTIETH BIRTHDAY' on the precious metal versions. Obv. as 4556. (Reverse design : Ian Rank-Broadley)
2008...£7
— Specimen in presentation folder (Issued: 54,746)......................................£10
— Proof *FDC* (in 2008 set, see PS93)* £15
— Proof in silver *FDC* (Issued: 7,446)..£60
— Proof piedfort in silver *FDC* (Edition: 5,000)...£90
— Proof in gold *FDC* (Issued: 867)...£1250
— Proof in platinum *FDC* (Issued: 54) £3600

4565   4566

4565 **Five pounds** (crown). 500th Anniversary of the accession of Henry VIII. R. A design inspired By a Holbein painting of King Henry VIII, set within a tressure and surrounded by the inscription 'THE ACCESSION OF HENRY VIII 1509' and the denomination 'FIVE POUNDS', with the edge inscription 'ROSA SINE SPINA' on the precious metal versions. Obv. as 4551. (Reverse design: John Bergdahl)
2009...£7
— Specimen in presentation folder (Edition: 100,000) £10
— Proof *FDC* (in 2009 set, see PS97)* £15
— Proof in silver *FDC* (Issued: 10,419))..£60
— Proof piedfort in silver *FDC* (Issued: 3,580) £90
— Proof in gold *FDC* (Issued: 1,130)..£1250
— Proof piedfort in platinum *FDC* (Edition: 100) £3600

4566 **Five pounds** (crown). Commemorating the three hundred-and fiftieth anniversary of the restoration of the Monarchy. R. A design featuring a crown, a spray of oak leaves, interlinked 'C's, the date '1660', the inscription 'RESTORATION OF THE MONARCHY' and the denomination 'FIVE POUNDS' with the edge inscription 'A QUIET AND PEACEFUL POSSESSION' on the precious metal versions. Obv. as 4551. (Reverse design: David Cornell)
2010...£7
— Specimen on presentation card (Edition: 150,000) £8
— Specimen in presentation folder (Edition: 50,000) £10
— Proof *FDC* (in 2010 set, see PS101)* £15
— Proof in silver *FDC* (Issued: 6,518)..£50
— Proof piedfort in silver *FDC* (Issued: 4,435) £90
— Proof in gold *FDC* (Issued: 1,182)..£1250
— Proof piedfort in platinum *FDC* (Edition: 100) £3600

* Coins marked thus were originally issued in Royal Mint sets.

4567

4567 Five pounds (crown). Royal Wedding Commemorative. R.A design featuring facing portraits of His Royal Highness Prince William and Miss Catherine Middleton with the inscription 'WILLIAM AND CATHERINE' above and the date '29 APRIL 2011 below. (Reverse design: Mark Richards)
2011
— Specimen in presentation folder (Issued: 250,000) £18
— Proof in silver *FDC* (Issued: 26,069)..£75
— Proof in silver with gold plating *FDC* (Issued: 7,451) £90
— Proof piedfort in silver *FDC* (Issued: 2,991)..£120
— Proof in gold *FDC* (Issued: 2,066) £1250
— Proof piedfort in platinum *FDC* (Edition: 200) £4500

4568

4568 Five pounds (crown). 90th Birthday of Prince Philip. R. A profile portrait of His Royal Highness The Duke of Edinburgh with the inscription 'PRINCE PHILIP 90TH BIRTHDAY ' and the denomination 'FIVE POUNDS' and the date '2011' (Reverse design: Mark Richards)
2011
— Specimen in presentation folder (Edition: 50,000)..£10
— Proof *FDC* (in 2011 set, see PS104)*..£15
— Proof in silver *FDC* (Issued: 4,599) £83
— Proof piedfort in silver *FDC* (Issued: 2,659)...£145
— Proof in gold *FDC* (Issued: 636) £1250
— Proof piedfort in platinum *FDC* (Edition: 90)..£4500

* Coins marked thus were originally issued in Royal Mint sets.

4569

4569 **Five pounds** (crown). Diamond Jubilee commemorative 2012. O. For the obverse impression, Our Effigy, inspired by the sculpture mounted in the entrance to the Supreme Court building on Parliament Square, with the inscription 'ELIZABETH. II. D. G. REG. F. D. FIVE POUNDS', and for the reverse an adaptation of Our Effigy first used on United Kingdom coins from 1953, with an olive branch and ribbon below, the date '2012' to the left and the inscription 'DIRIGE DEVS GRESSVS MEOS' to the right. With the edge inscription 'A VOW MADE GOOD' on the precious metal coins. (Obverse and reverse designs: Ian Rank-Broadley)

2012
- — Specimen in presentation folder £13
- — Proof *FDC* (in 2012 set, see PS107)* £10
- — Proof in silver *FDC* (Edition: 75,000 including coins in sets) £83
- — Proof in silver with gold plating *FDC* (Edition: 12,500) £100
- — Proof piedfort in silver *FDC* (Edition: 3,250) £145
- — Proof in gold *FDC* (Edition: 3,850) £1250
- — Proof piedfort in platinum *FDC* (Edition: 250)..£4500

4751

4751 **Five pounds** (crown). Coronation Anniversary commemorative 2013.R. In the centre The Imperial State Crown with the inscription 'TO REIGN AND SERVE' and 'A VOW MADE GOOD' (Reverse design: Emma Noble).

2013
- — Specimen in presentation folder £13
- — Proof *FDC* (in 2013 set, see PS109)* £10
- — Proof in silver *FDC* (Edition: 60,000 including coins in sets) £80
- — Proof in silver with gold plating *FDC* (Edition: 12,500) £100
- — Proof piedfort in silver *FDC* (Edition: 5,263 including coins in sets) £160
- — Proof in gold *FDC* (Edition: 2,060 including coins in sets)............................ £2400
- — Proof piedfort in platinum *FDC* (Edition: 150).. £6400

* Coins marked thus were originally issued in Royal Mint sets.

4752

4752 Five pounds (crown). Commemorative coin to mark the birth of a son to the Duke and
Duchess of Cambridge. R. A depiction of St. George armed, sitting on horseback, attacking
the dragon with a sword, and a broken spear upon the ground, and the date of the year.
(Reverse design: Benedetto Pistrucci).
2013
  —   Proof in silver *FDC* (Edition: 10,000) £80

4753

4753 Five pounds (crown) Commemorative coin to mark the christening of Prince George
of Cambridge. R. A deconstructed silver lily font incorporating cherubs and roses, with
a Baroque-style cartouche with the inscription 'DIEU ET MON DROIT' and ' TO
CELEBRATE THE CHRISTENING OF PRINCE GEORGE OF CAMBRIDGE 2013' in
the centre of the coin. (Reverse design: John Bergdahl).
2013
  —   Specimen in presentation folder £13
  —   Proof in silver FDC (Edition: 12,500) £80
  —   Proof piedfort in silver FDC (Edition: 2,500) £160
  —   Proof in gold FDC (Edition: 1,000) £2000
  —   Proof piedfort in platinum FDC (Edition: 100)................................. £6400

* Coins marked thus were originally issued in Royal Mint sets.

4754

4754   Five pounds (crown). Obverse design depicts the Royal Arms with the date '2013' below. R. The portrait of The Queen by Mary Gillick with the inscription 'ELIZABETH II DEI GRATIA REGINA F.D.' and the denomination 'FIVE POUNDS' below. (Obverse design: James Butler).

2013
— Proof in silver *FDC* (Edition: 5,000 in sets, see PSS53)* £100
— Proof piedfort in silver *FDC* (Edition: 3,000 in sets, see PSS54)* £200
— Proof in gold *FDC* (Edition: 500 in sets, see PGQPS)* £2400

4755

4755   Five pounds (crown). Obverse design depicts the Royal Arms with the date 2013' below. R. The portrait of The Queen by Arnold Machin with the inscription 'ELIZABETH II D: G REG: F: D: FIVE POUNDS'. (Obverse design: James Butler).

2013
— Proof in silver *FDC* (Edition: 5,000 in sets, see PSS53)* £100
— Proof piedfort in silver *FDC* (Edition: 3,000 in sets, see PSS54)* £200
— Proof in gold *FDC* (Edition: 500 in sets, see PGQPS)* £2400

4756   4757

4756 Five pounds (crown). Obverse design depicts the Royal Arms with the date '2013'
    below. R. The portrait of The Queen by Raphael Maklouf with the inscription
    'ELIZABETH II DEI. GRATIA. REGINA. F. D.' and the denomination 'FIVE
    POUNDS' below. (Obverse design: James Butler).
    2013
    — Proof in silver *FDC* (Edition: 5,000 in sets, see PSS53)* £100
    — Proof piedfort in silver *FDC* (Edition: 3,000 in sets, see PSS54)* £200
    — Proof in gold *FDC* (Edition: 500 in sets, see PGQPS)* £2400

4757 Five pounds (crown). Obverse design depicts the Royal Arms with the date '2013'
    below. R. The portrait of The Queen by Ian Rank-Broadley with the inscription
    'ELIZABETH II D. G. REG. F.D and the denomination 'FIVE POUNDS' below.
    (Obverse design: James Butler).
    2013
    — Proof in silver *FDC* (Edition: 5,000 in sets, see PSS53)* £100
    — Proof piedfort in silver *FDC* (Edition: 3,000 in sets, see PSS54)* £200
    — Proof in gold *FDC* (Edition: 500 in sets, see PGQPS)* £2400

4758

4758 Five pounds (crown). Queen Anne commemorative. R. The effigy pf Queen Anne
    enclosed by baroque decoration including the Royal Arms from the reign of Queen
    Anne and surrounded by the inscription 'QUEEN ANNE DEI GRATIA 1665-1714'
    (Reverse design: Mark Edwards).
    2014
    — Specimen in presentation folder £13
    — Proof *FDC* (in 2014 set, see PS112)* £10
    — Proof in silver *FDC* (Edition: 60,000 including coins in sets) £80
    — Proof in silver with gold plating *FDC* (Edition: 5,114) £100
    — Proof piedfort in silver *FDC* (Edition: 4,028 including coins in sets) £160
    — Proof in gold *FDC* (Edition: 2,060 including coins in sets) £2400
    — Proof piedfort in platinum *FDC* (Edition: 150) £6400

* Coins marked thus were originally issued in Royal Mint sets.

4759

4759 **Five pounds** (crown). Commemorative coin to mark the first birthday of Prince
George of Cambridge. R. The four Quarterings of Our Royal Arms each contained in
a shield and arranged in saltire with, in the intervening spaces, a Rose, a Thistle, both
slipped and leaved, a sprig of shamrock and a Leek, in the centre the Crown and in the
base the date of the year. (Reverse design: Edgar Fuller)
2014
— Proof in silver *FDC* (Edition: 7,500) £80

4760   4761

4760 **Five pounds** (crown). Celebrating British Landmarks. R. A design depicting the
head of one of the lions in Trafalgar Square with Nelson's Column in the background
and the inscription 'FIVE POUNDS' (Reverse design: Glyn Davies and Laura Clancy)
2014
— Proof in silver *FDC* with colour printing (Edition: 5,000 see PSS59)

4761 **Five pounds** (crown). Celebrating British Landmarks. R. A design depicting a view
of the Elizabeth Tower with the inscription 'FIVE POUNDS' (Reverse design:
Glyn Davies and Laura Clancy)
2014
— Proof in silver *FDC* with colour printing (Edition: 5,000 see PSS59)

* Coins marked thus were originally issued in Royal Mint sets.

4762   4763

4762   **Five pounds** (crown). Celebrating British Landmarks. R. A design depicting Tower Bridge with the inscription 'FIVE POUNDS' (Reverse design: Glyn Davies and Laura Clancy)
       2014
       —   Proof in silver *FDC* with colour printing (Edition: 5,000   see PSS59)

4763   **Five pounds** (crown). Celebrating British Landmarks. R. A design depicting the Victoria Memorial with Buckingham Palace in the background and the inscription 'FIVE POUNDS' (Reverse design: Glyn Davies and Laura Clancy)
       2014
       —   Proof in silver FDC with colour printing (Edition: 5,000   see PSS59)

4640

4640   **Ten pounds** (five ounce). Diamond Jubilee commemorative 2012. O. For the obverse impression, Our Effigy, inspired by the sculpture mounted in the entrance to the Supreme Court building on Parliament Square, with the inscription 'ELIZABETH. II. D. G. REG. F. D. TEN POUNDS', and for the reverse an enthroned representation of Ourself surrounded by the inscription 'DILECTA REGNO MCMLII – MMXII' (Obverse and reverse design: Ian Rank-Broadley)
       2012
       —   Proof in silver *FDC* (Edition: 1,952) £350
       —   Proof in gold *FDC* (Edition: 250) £7500
       Illustration shown at reduced size – actual coin diameter 65 mm.

* *Coins marked thus were originally issued in Royal Mint sets.*

4641

4641 **Ten pounds** (five ounce). Coronation Anniversary. R. In the foreground the Orb and
Sceptre resting upon the Coronation Robe with the arches of Westminster Abbey
in the background with the inscription 'HER MAJESTY QUEEN ELIZABETH II
CORONATION ANNIVERSARY' (Reverse design: Jonathan Olliffe).
2013
— Proof in silver (0.999) *FDC* (Edition: 1,953)... £450
— Proof in gold (0.9999) *FDC* (Edition: 129)..£9500
Illustration shown at reduced size – actual coin diameter 63mm

4642

4642 **Ten pounds** (five ounce) Commemorative coin to mark the christening of Prince
George of Cambridge. R. A deconstructed silver lily font incorporating cherubs and
roses, with a Baroque-style cartouche with the inscription 'DIEU ET MON DROIT'
and ' TO CELEBRATE THE CHRISTENING OF PRINCE GEORGE OF
CAMBRIDGE 2013' in the centre of the coin. (Reverse design: John Bergdahl).
2013
— Proof in silver (0.999) *FDC* (Edition: 1,660)... £450
— Proof in gold (0.9999) *FDC* (Edition: 150)..£9500
Illustration shown at reduced size – actual coin diameter 63mm

* *Coins marked thus were originally issued in Royal Mint sets.*

4643

4643 Ten pounds (five ounce). 100th Anniversary of the outbreak of the First World War.
R. A depiction of a lion behind the figure of Britannia holding a shield and a trident,
watching over departing ships from a cliff top, with the inscription 'THE FIRST
WORLD WAR 1914 1918' and the date at the base of the coin. (0.999 fine silver.)
(Reverse design: John Bergdahl)
2014
—   Proof in silver (0.999) *FDC* (Edition: 1,300).. £395
—   Proof in gold (0.9999) *FDC* (Edition: 100)..£7500

* Coins marked thus were originally issued in Royal Mint sets.

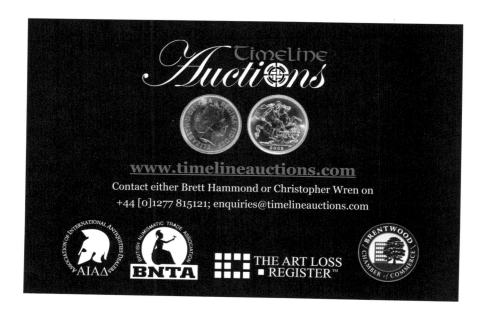

4770

4770 Twenty pounds. R. A depiction of St. George armed, sitting on horseback, attacking the dragon with a sword, and a broken spear upon the ground and the date of the year. (0.999 fine silver) (Reverse design: Benedetto Pistrucci).

2013

— Bu in silver (Edition: 250,000)...£20

4771

4771 Twenty pounds. R. A depiction of a lion behind the figure of Britannia holding a shield and a trident, watching over departing ships from a cliff top, with the inscription 'THE FIRST WORLD WAR 1914 1918' and the date at the base of the coin. (0.999 fine silver) (Reverse design: John Bergdahl)

2014

— Bu in silver (Edition: 250,000)...£20

4775 One hundred pounds. World War I R. A depiction of Lord Kitchener pointing above the inscription 'YOUR COUNTRY NEEDS YOU' and the inscription 'THE FIRST WORLD WAR 1914-1918' and the date '2014' with the edge inscription 'THE LAMPS ARE GOING OUT ALL OVER EUROPE' (Reverse design: John Bergdahl).

2014

— Proof in Platinum *FDC*

Illustration shown at reduced size – actual coin diameter 100mm

* *Coins marked thus were originally issued in Royal Mint sets.*

4780

4780 **Five hundred pounds** (one kilo). Diamond Jubilee commemorative 2012. O. For the
obverse impression, Our Effigy, inspired by the sculpture mounted in the entrance to the
Supreme Court building on Parliament Square, with the inscription 'ELIZABETH. II. D.
G. REG. F. D. 500 POUNDS', and for the reverse a full achievement of the Royal Arms
based on those mounted on the front gates of Buckingham Palace with the date '2012'
below. (Obverse and reverse design: Ian Rank-Broadley)
2012
—   Proof in silver *FDC* (Edition: 1,250) £2000
Illustration shown at reduced size – actual coin diameter 100 mm.

4781 **Five hundred pounds** (one kilo). R. Coronation commemorative 2013. R. In the
foreground the Orb and Sceptre with the St. Edward's Crown behind surrounding by
flowers representing the constituent parts of the United Kingdom and in the background a
ribbon showing the '2nd JUNE 1953' with the inscription 'QUEEN ELIZABETH II' and
'THE 60TH ANNIVERSARY OF THE CORONATION' (Reverse design: John Bergdahl)
2013
—   Proof in silver *FDC* (0.999) (Edition: 400)...£2600

4782

4782 **Five hundred pounds** (1 kilo of fine silver). Commemorative coin to mark the
christening of Prince George of Cambridge. R. A deconstructed silver lily font
incorporating cherubs and roses, with a Baroque-style cartouche with the inscription
'DIEU ET MON DROIT' and 'TO CELEBRATE THE CHRISTENING OF PRINCE
GEORGE OF CAMBRIDGE 2013'in the centre of the coin. (Reverse design:
John Bergdahl).
2013
—   Proof in silver (0.999) *FDC* (Edition:500)... £2000
Illustration shown at reduced size – actual coin diameter 100mm

* *Coins marked thus were originally issued in Royal Mint sets.*

4783

4783 **Five hundred pounds.** (1 kilo of fine silver). World War 1. R. A design depicting
British soldiers marching through no man's land with the figure of a British with
rifle and helmet in the foreground and the dates '1914-1918' at the base of the coin.
(Reverse design: Michael Sandle).
2014
— Proof in silver (0.999) *FDC* (Edition: 430)...£2000
Illustration shown at reduced size – actual coin diameter 100mm

4790

4790 **One thousand pounds** (one kilo). Diamond Jubilee commemorative 2012. O. For the
obverse impression, Our Effigy, inspired by the sculpture mounted in the entrance to the
Supreme Court building on Parliament Square, with the inscription 'ELIZABETH. II. D.
G. REG. F. D. 1000 POUNDS', and for the reverse a full achievement of the Royal Arms
based on those mounted on the front gates of Buckingham Palace with the date '2012'
below. (Reverse design:
2012
— Proof in gold *FDC* (Edition: 60) £60000
Illustration shown at reduced size – actual coin diameter 100mm

4791 **One thousand pounds** (One kilo). Coronation commemorative 2013. R. In the
foreground the Orb and Sceptre with the St. Edward's Crown behind surrounding by
flowers representing the constituent parts of the United Kingdom and in the background
a ribbon showing the '2nd JUNE 1953' with the inscription 'QUEEN ELIZABETH II'
and 'THE 60TH ANNIVERSARY OF THE CORONATION' (Reverse design:
John Bergdahl)
2013
— Proof in gold *FDC* (0.9999) (Edition: 27) £60000

* Coins marked thus were originally issued in Royal Mint sets.

4792

4792 One thousand pounds (1 kilo of fine gold). Commemorative coin to mark the
christening of Prince George of Cambridge. R. A deconstructed silver lily font
incorporating cherubs and roses, with a Baroque-style cartouche with the inscription
'DIEU ET MON DROIT' and 'TO CELEBRATE THE CHRISTENING OF PRINCE
GEORGE OF CAMBRIDGE 2013'in the centre of the coin. (Reverse design:
John Bergdahl).
2013
—   Proof in gold *FDC* (0.9999) (Edition:22)..£50000
Illustration shown at reduced size – actual coin diameter 100mm

4793

4793 One thousand pounds. (1 kilo of fine gold). World War 1. R. A design depicting
British soldiers marching through no man's land with the figure of a British with
rifle and helmet in the foreground and the dates '1914-1918' at the base of the coin.
(Reverse design: Michael Sandle).
2014
—   Proof in gold *FDC* (0.9999) (Edition: 25)..£45000
Illustration shown at reduced size – actual coin diameter 100mm

* Coins marked thus were originally issued in Royal Mint sets.

GOLD SOVEREIGN ISSUES

Obverse portrait by Ian Rank-Broadley

4445   4446

4445 Quarter sovereign. R. The image of St George armed, sitting on horseback, attacking
the dragon with a sword, and a broken spear upon the ground, and the date of the year.
(Reverse design: Benedetto Pistrucci)
2009 Bullion type (Edition: 50,000)..£110
—   Proof FDC (Issued: 13,495 including coins in sets)...£130
2010 Bullion type (Edition: 250,000)..£110
—   Proof FDC (Issued: 6,007 including coins in sets)...£130
2011 Bullion type (Edition: 50,000)..£110
—   Proof FDC (Issued: 7,764 including coins in sets)...£130
2013 Bullion type
—   Proof FDC (Edition: 5,645 including coins in sets)*
2014 Bullion type
—   Proof FDC (Edition: 4,575 including coins in sets)* £110

4446 Quarter sovereign. R. The image of St George on horseback, attacking the dragon with a
lance, with date of the year to the left. (Reverse design: Paul Day)
2012 Bullion type (Edition: 250,000) £80
—   Proof *FDC* (Edition: 10,744 including coins in sets)..£110

Obverse portrait by Arnold Machin

4205

4205 Half-sovereign. R. The image of St George armed, sitting on horseback, attacking the
dragon with a sword, and a broken spear upon the ground, and the date of the year.
(Reverse design: Benedetto Pistrucci)
1980 Proof *FDC* (Issued: 76.700). £125   1983 Proof *FDC* (Issued: 19,710)** £125
1982 Unc .... £100   1984 Proof *FDC* (Issued: 12,410) £125
—   Proof *FDC* (Issued: 19,090).. £125

* Coins marked thus were originally issued in Royal Mint sets.
** Numbers include coins sold in sets

Obverse portrait by Raphael Maklouf

4276   4277

4276 Half-sovereign. R. St. George (as 4205)

1985 Proof *FDC* (Issued: 9,951)... £160	1992 Proof *FDC* (Issued: 3,783) £175
1986 Proof *FDC* (Issued: 4,575)... £160	1993 Proof *FDC* (Issued: 2,910) £175
1987 Proof *FDC* (Issued: 8,187)... £160	1994 Proof *FDC* (Issued: 5,000) £150
1988 Proof *FDC* (Issued: 7,074)... £160	1995 Proof *FDC* (Issued: 4,900) £150
1990 Proof *FDC* (Issued: 4,231)... £175	1996 Proof *FDC* (Issued: 5,730) £150
1991 Proof *FDC* (Issued: 3,588)... £175	1997 Proof *FDC* (Issued: 7,500) £150

4277 Half-sovereign 500th Anniversary of Sovereign. For the obverse impression a representation Of Ourself as at Our Coronation, seated in King Edward's Chair and having received the Sceptre with the Cross and the Rod with the Dove, all within the circumscription 'ELIZABETH. II.DEI.GRA.REG.FID.DEF' and for the reverse a Shield of Our Royal Arms ensigned by an open Royal Crown, the whole superimposed upon a double Rose, and with the circumscription 'ANNIVERSARY OF THE GOLD SOVEREIGN 1489-1989' (Designs: Bernald Sindall)

1989 Proof *FDC* (Issued: 8,888) £400

Obverse portrait by Ian Rank-Broadley

4440   4441   4442

4440 Half sovereign. R. St.George

1998 Proof *FDC* (Issued: 6,147)... £175	2004 Bullion type (Issued: 34,924) £140
1999 Proof *FDC* (Issued: 7,500)... £175	— Proof *FDC* (Issued: 4,446) £175
2000 Bullion type (Issued: 146,822). £140	2006 Bullion type £140
— Proof *FDC* (Issued: 7,458).... £175	— Proof *FDC* (Issued: 4,173) £175
2001 Bullion type (Issued: 94,763) .£140	2007 Bullion type (Edition: 75,000)........ £140
— Proof *FDC* (Issued: 4,596).... £175	— Proof *FDC* (Issued: 2,442) £175
2003 Bullion type (Issued: 47,818) £140	2008 Bullion type (Edition: 75,000)........ £140
— Proof *FDC* (Issued: 4,868).... £175	— Proof *FDC* (Issued: 2,465) £175

4441 Half sovereign R. The Shield of Arms of Our United Kingdom of Great Britain and Northern Ireland within an open wreath of laurel and ensigned by Our Royal Crown and beneath the date of the year. (Reverse design: Timothy Noad)

2002 Bullion type (Issued: 61,347)...£150

—   Proof *FDC* (Issued: 10,000)..£250

4442 Half sovereign. R. A depiction of St George, carrying a shield and a sword, slaying the dragon, with the date '2005' beneath the wing of the dragon.(Reverse design: Timothy Noad)

2005 Bullion type (Issued: 30,299)...£150

—   Proof *FDC* (Issued: 5,011) £250

* Coins marked thus were originally issued in Royal Mint sets.

4443

4443 Half sovereign. R. St George. Based on the original design of 1893 with reduced
ground below design and larger exergue with no BP initials
2009 Bullion type (Edition: 50,000)..£165
—   Proof *FDC* (Issued: 5,412 including coins in sets) £225
2010 Bullion type (Edition: 250,000)...£165
—   Proof *FDC* (Issued: 5,370 including coins in sets) £225
2011 Bullion type (Edition: 50,000)..£160
—   Proof *FDC* (Issued 5,287 including coins in sets)................................£250
2013 Bullion type
—   BU (Edition: 125 in sets, see PGS70)
—   Proof *FDC* (Edition: 4,795 including coins in sets)*
2014 Bullion type
—   BU (Edition: 9,900)..£170
—   Proof *FDC* (Edition: 4,075 including coins in sets)..............................£195

4444

4444 Half sovereign. R. The image of St George on horseback, attacking the dragon with a lance,
with date of the year to the left. (Reverse design: Paul Day)
2012 Bullion type (Edition: 250,000) £175
—   Proof *FDC* (Edition: 4,894 including coins in sets) £225

Obverse portrait by Arnold Machin

4204

4204 Sovereign. R. The image of St George armed, sitting on horseback, attacking the dragon
with a sword, and a broken spear upon the ground, and the date of the year.(Reverse
design: Benedetto Pistrucci)

1974 Unc £225	1981 Unc.................................. £225
1976 Unc £225	— Proof *FDC* (Issued: 32,960) £250
1976 VIP Proof *FDC*......*Extremely rare*	1982 Unc.................................. £225
1978 Unc £225	— Proof *FDC* (Issued: 20,000) £250
1979 Unc £225	1983 Proof *FDC* (Issued: 21,250)** £250
— Proof *FDC* (Issued: 50,000) £250	1984 Proof *FDC* (Issued: 12,880) £250
1980 Unc £225	
— Proof *FDC* (Issued: 81,200) £250	

* Coins marked thus were originally issued in Royal Mint sets.

Obverse portrait by Raphael Maklouf

4271   4272

4271 Sovereign. R. St. George (as 4204)

1985 Proof *FDC* (Issued: 11,393) . £300
1986 Proof *FDC* (Issued: 5,079)... £300
1987 Proof *FDC* (Issued: 9,979)... £300
1988 Proof *FDC* (Issued: 7,670)... £300
1990 Proof *FDC* (Issued: 4,767)... £350
1991 Proof *FDC* (Issued: 4,713)... £350

1992 Proof *FDC* (Issued: 4,772) £350
1993 Proof *FDC* (Issued: 4,349) £400
1994 Proof *FDC* (Issued: 4,998) £350
1995 Proof *FDC* (Issued: 7,500) £325
1996 Proof *FDC* (Issued: 7,500) £325
1997 Proof *FDC* (Issued: 7,500) £325

4272 Sovereign. 500th Anniversary of Sovereign. For the obverse impression a representation Of Ourself as at Our Coronation, seated in King Edward's Chair and having received the Sceptre with the Cross and the Rod with the Dove, all within the circumscription 'ELIZABETH.II.DEI.GRA.REG.FID.DEF' and for the reverse a Shield of Our Royal Arms ensigned by an open Royal Crown, the whole superimposed upon a double Rose, and with the circumscription 'ANNIVERSARY OF THE GOLD SOVEREIGN 1489-1989' (Designs: Bernald Sindall)
1989 Proof *FDC* (Issued: 10,535) £1200

Obverse portrait by Ian Rank-Broadley

4430

4430 Sovereign. R. St.George

1998 Proof *FDC* (Issued: 10,000) . £325
1999 Proof *FDC* (Issued: 10,000) . £350
2000 Bullion type (Issued: 129,069) .£225
— Proof *FDC* (Issued: 9,909).... £325
2001 Bullion type (Issued: 49,462) £225
— Proof *FDC* (Issued: 8,915).... £325
2003 Bullion type (Issued: 43,230) £225
— Proof *FDC* (Issued: 12,433).. £325

2004 Bullion type (Issued: 30,688) £225
— Proof *FDC* (Issued: 10,175) £325
2006 Bullion type £225
— Proof *FDC* (Issued: 9,195) £325
2007 Bullion type (Edition: 75,000)........£225
— Proof *FDC* (Issued: 8,199) £325
2008 Bullion type (Edition: 75,000)........£225
— Proof *FDC* (Edition: 12,500)...........£325

* Coins marked thus were originally issued in Royal Mint sets.
Where numbers of coins issued or the Edition limit is quoted, these refer to individual coins. Additional coins were included in sets which are listed in the appropriate section.

4431   4433   4434

4431 Sovereign R. The Shield of Arms of Our United Kingdom of Great Britain and Northern
Ireland within an open wreath of laurel and ensigned by Our Royal Crown and beneath
the date of the year. (Reverse design: Timothy Noad)
2002 Bullion type (Issued: 75,264) £300
— Proof *FDC* (Issued: 12,500) £400

4432 Sovereign R. A depiction of St George, carrying a shield and a sword, slaying the dragon,
with the date '2005' beneath the wing of the dragon.(Reverse design: Timothy Noad)
2005 Bullion type (Issued: 45,542) £300
— Proof *FDC* (Issued: 12,500) £400

4433 Sovereign. R. St George. Based on the original design of 1820 with the plumed
helmet without its streamer.
2009 Bullion type (Edition: 75,000)...£325
— Proof *FDC* (Issued: 9,770 including coins in sets)...£400
2010 Bullion type (Edition: 250,000)...£325
— Proof *FDC* (Issued: 8,828 including coins in sets)...£400
2011 Bullion type (Edition: 250,000)...£325
— Proof *FDC* (Edition: 15,000 including coins in sets) £450
2013 Bullion type
— BU (Edition: 125 in sets, see PGS70)
— Proof *FDC* (Edition: 10,295 including coins in sets)
2014 Bullion type
— BU (Edition: 15,000) £325
— Proof *FDC* (Edition: 9,725 including coins in sets) £390

4433ASovereign. R. St George as 4433 above but with 'I' mint mark on reverse for coins
struck in India.
2013 BU

4434 Sovereign. R. The image of St George on horseback, attacking the dragon with a lance,
with date of the year to the left. (Reverse design: Paul Day)
2012 Bullion type (Edition: 250,000)...£275
— Proof *FDC* (Edition: 8,144 including coins in sets) £400

* Coins marked thus were originally issued in Royal Mint sets.

Obverse portrait by Arnold Machin

4203

4203   Two pounds R. The image of St George armed, sitting on horseback, attacking the dragon
with a sword, and a broken spear upon the ground, and the date of the year.(Reverse design:
Benedetto Pistrucci)

1980 Proof *FDC* (see PGS01)* ....£525   1983 Proof *FDC* (Issued: 12,500) ** £525
1982 Proof *FDC* (see PGS03)* £525

Obverse portrait by Raphael Maklouf

4261

4261   Two pounds. R. St. George (as 4203)

1985 Proof *FDC* (see PGS06)* ....£525   1991 Proof *FDC* (Issued: 620) £525
1987 Proof *FDC* (Issued: 1,801) ....£525   1992 Proof *FDC* (Issued: 476) £525
1988 Proof *FDC* (Issued: 1,551) ....£525   1993 Proof *FDC* (Issued: 414) £525
1990 Proof *FDC* (Issued: 716) ....£525   1996 Proof *FDC* (see PGS24)* £525

4262

4262   Two pounds 500th Anniversary of Sovereign. For the obverse impression a representation Of
Ourself as at Our Coronation, seated in King Edward's Chair and having received the Sceptre
with the Cross and the Rod with the Dove, all within the circumscription 'ELIZABETH.
II.DEI.GRA.REG.FID.DEF' and for the reverse a Shield of Our Royal Arms ensigned by an
open Royal Crown, the whole superimposed upon a double Rose, and with the circumscription
'ANNIVERSARY OF THE GOLD SOVEREIGN 1489-1989' (Designs: Bernald Sindall)
1989 Proof *FDC* (Issued: 2,000) £900

* *Coins marked thus were originally issued in Royal Mint sets.*

Obverse portrait by Ian Rank-Broadley

4420

4420 Two pounds. R. St. George
  1998 Proof *FDC* (see PGS28)* £500
  2003 Proof *FDC* (see PGS38)* £500
  2007 Proof *FDC* (see PGS46)* £500

  2000 Proof *FDC* (see PGS32)* £500
  2006 Proof *FDC* (see PGS44)* £500
  2008 Proof *FDC* (see PGS49)* £500

4421   4422   4423

4421 Two pounds. R. The Shield of Arms of Our United Kingdom of Great Britain and
  Northern Ireland within an open wreath of laurel and ensigned by Our Royal Crown and
  beneath the date of the year. (Reverse design: Timothy Noad)
  2002 Proof *FDC* (see PGS36)* £700

4422 Two pounds. R. A depiction of St George, carrying a shield and a sword, slaying the
  dragon, with the date '2005' beneath the wing of the dragon.(Reverse design:
  Timothy Noad)
  2005 Proof *FDC* (see PGS42)* £700

4423 Two pounds. R. St George. Based on the original design of 1820 with greater detail on
  the dragon.
  2009 Proof FDC (see PGS52)* £600
  2010 Proof FDC (Edition: 2,750 in sets)* £600
  2011 Proof FDC (Edition: 2,950 in sets)* £1000
  2013 BU (Edition: 125 in sets, see PGS70)
  —   Proof FDC (Edition: 1,895 in sets)*
  2014 BU (Edition: 1,300) £650
  —   Proof FDC (Edition:)

* *Coins marked thus were originally issued in Royal Mint sets.*

4424

4424 Two pounds. R. The image of St George on horseback, attacking the dragon with a lance, with date of the year to the left. (Reverse design: Paul Day)

2012 BU (Edition: 60 in three coin set, see PGS6)* £1000

— Proof *FDC* (Edition: 1,944 including coins in sets)*

Obverse portrait by Arnold Machin

4201

4201 Five pounds. R. The image of St George armed, sitting on horseback, attacking the dragon with a sword, and a broken spear upon the ground, and the date of the year.(Reverse design: Benedetto Pistrucci)

1980 Proof *FDC* (see PGS01)* ... £1250   1982 Proof *FDC* (see PGS03)* £1250

1981 Proof *FDC* (Issued: 5,400) ** £1250   1984 Proof *FDC* (Issued: 905) £1250

4202 As 4201 but, 'U' in a circle to left of date

1984 (Issued: 15,104) *Unc* £1250

Obverse portrait by Raphael Maklouf

4251

4251 Five pounds. R. St. George (as 4201)

1985 Proof *FDC* (see PGS06)* ... £1250   1990 Proof *FDC* (see PGS12)* £1250

1991 Proof *FDC* (see PGS14)* ... £1250   1992 Proof *FDC* (see PGS16)* £1250

1993 Proof *FDC* (see PGS18)* ... £1250   1994 Proof *FDC* (see PGS20)* £1250

1995 Proof *FDC* (see PGS22)* ... £1250   1996 Proof *FDC* (see PGS24)* £1250

1997 Proof *FDC* (see PGS26)* .. £1250

* *Coins marked thus were originally issued in Royal Mint sets.*

4252 Five pounds R. St George, 'U' in a circle to left of date.

1985 (Issued: 13,626)..................£1250	1993 (Issued: 906)................................£1250
1986 (Issued: 7,723)....................£1250	1994 (Issued: 1,000)..............................£1250
1990 (Issued: 1,226)....................£1250	1995 (Issued: 1,000)..............................£1250
1991 (Issued: 976)......................£1250	1996 (Issued: 901)................................£1250
1992 (Issued: 797)......................£1250	1997 (Issued: 802)................................£1250

4253

4253 Five pounds Uncouped portrait of Queen Elizabeth II. As illustration. R. St. George, 'U' in a circle to left of date.

1987 (Issued: 5,694)....................£1250   1988 (Issued: 3,315)...............................£1250

4254

4254 Five pounds 500th Anniversary of Sovereign. For the obverse impression a representation Of Ourself as at Our Coronation, seated in King Edward's Chair and having received the Sceptre with the Cross and the Rod with the Dove, all within the circumscription 'ELIZABETH.II.DEI.GRA.REG.FID.DEF' and for the reverse a Shield of Our Royal Arms ensigned by an open Royal Crown, the whole superimposed upon a double Rose, and with the circumscription 'ANNIVERSARY OF THE GOLD SOVEREIGN 1489-1989' (Designs: Bernald Sindall)

1989 (Issued: 2,937)..£1650

—   Proof *FDC* (see PGS10)*...£2000

* Coins marked thus were originally issued in Royal Mint sets.

Obverse portrait by Ian Rank-Broadley

4400

4400 **Five pounds.** R. St.George

1998 Proof *FDC* (see PGS28)*... £1250
1999 Proof *FDC* (see PGS30)*... £1250
2000 Bullion type........................ £1250
— Proof *FDC* (see PGS32)*.... £1250
2001 Proof *FDC* (see PGS34)*... £1250
2003 Unc (Issued: 812) £1250
— Proof *FDC* (see PGS38)*.... £1250

2004 Unc (Issued: 1,000)...................... £1250
— Proof *FDC* (see PGS40)* £1250
2006 Unc (Issued: 731).......................... £1250
— Proof *FDC* (see PGS44)* £1250
2007 Unc (Issued: 768).......................... £1250
— Proof *FDC* (see PGS46)* £1250
2008 Unc (Issued: 750).......................... £1250
— Proof *FDC* (see PGS49)* £1250

4401 4402

4401 **Five pounds.** R. The Shield of Arms of Our United Kingdom of Great Britain and Northern Ireland within an open wreath of laurel and ensigned by Our Royal Crown and beneath the date of the year. (Reverse design: Timothy Noad)

2002 Unc (Issued: 1,370) £1300
— Proof *FDC* (see PGS36)* £1500

4402 **Five pounds.** R. A depiction of St George, carrying a shield and a sword, slaying the dragon, with the date '2005' beneath the wing of the dragon.(Reverse design: Timothy Noad)

2005 Unc (Issued: 936) £1300
— Proof *FDC* (see PGS42)* £1500

* Coins marked thus were originally issued in Royal Mint sets.

4403

4403 **Five pounds.** ℞. St George. Based on the original pattern piece of 1820 with the designer's name, 'PISTRUCCI', shown in full in the exergue, and with a broader rim.

2009 BU (Issued: 1,000) ....£1550 — Proof *FDC* (see PGS52)*.................£1550
2010 BU (Issued: 1,000) ....£1550 — Proof *FDC* (Edition: 2,000 in sets)* £1550
2011 BU (Issued: 657) ....£2100 — Proof *FDC* (Edition: 2,000 in sets)* £2100
2013 BU (Edition: 750).................£1900 — Proof *FDC* (Edition: 1,000 in sets)*
2014 BU (Edition 1,000)...............£1450 — Proof *FDC* (Edition:)

4404

4404 **Five pounds.** ℞. The image of St George on horseback, attacking the dragon with a lance, with date of the year to the left. (Reverse design: Paul Day)

2012 BU (Edition: 1,250)..£2000
— Proof *FDC* (Edition: 999 coins in sets)*

4410 **Five pounds.** ℞. St. George, 'U' in a circle to left of date

1998 (Issued: 825) ....£1250   2000 (Issued: 994) £1250
1999 (Issued: 970) ....£1250   2001 (Issued: 1,000) £1250

* Coins marked thus were originally issued in Royal Mint sets.

BRITANNIA COIN ISSUES

In 1987 the Mint decided to enter the market for bullion coins and launched a series of four gold coins with weights that corresponded to those already issued by a number of gold producing countries such as Canada, South Africa and China. The plan was to sell bullion quality coins in quantity to trade customers and investors at modest premiums over the ruling gold market price, and also to sell proof versions in limited editions to collectors.

Due to market reaction, particularly from the Far East, silver rather than copper was alloyed with the gold in 1990 in an effort to increase demand but in the absence of sales figures, it appears that the major interest is now to be found among collectors of the proof collector versions.

To mark the 10th anniversary of the first design, silver coins struck in Britannia silver (0.958) were introduced in the same four weights. Again the main interest seems to have been among collectors of the proof versions although the one ounce silver bullion coin of £2 face value has proved popular as silver prices have risen.

There are some attractive and different interpretations of Britannia with the gold and silver issues sharing the same designs as they are changed. The range of designs thus far are shown below, and the complete sets are listed in the appropriate sections towards the end of the catalogue.

BRITANNIA SILVER

Obverse portrait by Ian Rank-Broadley

4675   4680

4675 **Britannia. Five pence.** R. (1/40 oz of fine silver) A design of the standing figure of Britannia baring a trident and shield, with a lion at her feet, set against the backdrop of a globe, and with the inscription 'BRITANNIA 999 1/40 OZ FINE SILVER 2014' (Reverse design: Jody Clark)
2014 — Proof in silver *FDC* (0.999) (Edition: 2,750 including coins in sets)*
Illustration shown larger than actual coin diameter of 8mm

4680 **Britannia. Ten pence.** (1/20 oz of fine silver) (Previously listed as 4550) R. Seated figure of Britannia holding a trident with a shield at her side and an owl upon her knee with the word 'BRITANNIA' and the date of the year above and the inscription '1/20 OUNCE FINE SILVER' below the figure of Britannia. (Reverse design: Robert Hunt)
2013 — Proof in silver *FDC* (0.999) (Edition: 12,000 including coins in sets)*

4681 **Britannia. Ten pence.** (1/20 oz of fine silver) R. A design of the standing figure of Britannia baring a trident and shield, with a lion at her feet, set against the backdrop of a globe, and with the inscription ' BRITANNIA 999 1/20 OZ FINE SILVER 2014' (Reverse design: Jody Clark)
2014 — Proof in silver *FDC* (0.999) (Edition: 3,300 including coins in sets)*

* *Coins marked thus were originally issued in Royal Mint sets.*

Obverse portrait by Raphael Maklouf

4300C

4300C **Britannia. Twenty pence.** (1/10 oz of fine silver) 10th Anniversary of Britannia issue R. The figure of Britannia standing in a chariot drawn along the seashore by two horses, with the word 'BRITANNIA', the inscription. '1/10 OUNCE FINE SILVER' and the date of the year. (Reverse design: Philip Nathan).
1997 Proof *FDC* (Issued: 8,686, plus coins issued in sets, see PSB01) £20

Obverse portrait by Ian Rank-Broadley

4530   4531   4532   4534

4530 **Britannia. Twenty pence.** (1/10 oz of fine silver) R. The figure of Britannia standing upon a rock in the sea, her right hand grasping a trident and her left hand resting on a shield and holding an olive branch, with the word 'BRITANNIA', the date of the year, and the inscription '1/10 OUNCE FINE SILVER'. (Reverse design: Philip Nathan). (See 4500)
1998 — Proof *FDC* (Issued: 2,724, plus coins issued in sets, see PSB02) £20
2006 BU version £15
2012 — Proof *FDC* (Edition: 2,600 in sets see PBS14)*

4531 **Britannia. Twenty pence.** (1/10 oz of fine silver) R. The figure of Britannia, as guardian, with a shield in her left hand and a trident in her right hand, accompanied by a lion and, against the background of a wave motif, the words '1/10 OUNCE FINE SILVER' to the left and 'BRITANNIA' and the date of the year to the right. (Reverse design: Philip Nathan).
2001 — Proof *FDC* (Issued: 826, plus coins issued in sets, see PSB03) £20

4532 **Britannia. Twenty pence.** (1/10 oz fine silver) R. Helmeted head of Britannia with, to the left, the word 'BRITANNIA' and, to the right, the inscription '1/10 OUNCE FINE SILVER' and the date of the year, the whole being overlaid with a wave pattern. (Reverse design: Philip Nathan)
2003 — Proof *FDC* (Issued: 1,179, plus coins issued in sets, see PBS04) £20

4533 **Britannia. Twenty pence.** (Previously listed as 4515) (1/10 oz of fine silver) R. Seated figure of Britannia facing to the left holding a trident with a shield at her side, with the word 'BRITANNIA', the inscription '1/10 OUNCE FINE SILVER' and the date of the year. (Reverse design: Philip Nathan)
2005 — Proof *FDC** (Issued: 913, plus coins issued in sets, see PBS06) £20

4534 **Britannia. Twenty pence.** (1/10 oz of fine silver) R. Seated figure of Britannia facing right holding a trident in her right hand and a sprig of olive in the left hand with a lion at her feet with the inscription '1/10 OUNCE FINE SILVER' and the word 'BRITANNIA' and the date of the year (Reverse design: Christopher Le Brun)
2007 — Proof *FDC* (Issued: 901, plus coins issued in sets, see PBS08) £20

4535 **Britannia. Twenty pence.** (1/10 oz of fine silver) R. A Standing figure of Britannia holding a trident with a shield at her side, the folds of her dress transforming into a wave, with the word 'BRITANNIA' and the date of the year and the inscription '1/10 OUNCE FINE SILVER' (Reverse design: John Bergdahl). (See 4506)
2008 — Proof *FDC* (Edition: 2,500, plus coins issued in sets, see PBS1010)................£20

* Coins marked thus were originally issued in Royal Mint sets.

4536   4537   4539

4536 Britannia. Twenty pence. (1/10 oz fine silver) R. Standing figure of Britannia in horse
drawn chariot. (See 4501)
2009 — Proof *FDC* (Edition; 3,500 including coins in sets)..£25

4537 Britannia. Twenty pence. (1/10 oz fine silver) R. A design depicting a profile bust of
Britannia wearing a helmet, accompanied by the name 'BRITANNIA', the inscription
'1/10 OUNCE FINE SILVER' and the date '2010'. (Reverse design: Suzie Zamit)
2010 Proof *FDC* (Edition: 8,000 including coins in sets)..£25

4538 Britannia. Twenty pence. (1/10 oz fine silver) R. A design depicting a seated figure of
Britannia set against a background of a rippling Union Flag accompanied by the words '1/10
OUNCE FINE SILVER BRITANNIA' and the date '2011'. (Reverse design: David Mach)
2011 — Proof *FDC* (Edition: 6,000 including coins in sets)

4539 Britannia. Twenty pence. (1/10 oz of fine silver).R. Seated figure of Britannia holding
a trident with a shield at her side and an owl upon her knee with the word 'BRITANNIA'
and the date of the year above and the inscription '1/10 OUNCE FINE SILVER' below
the figure of Britannia. (Reverse design: Robert Hunt)
2013 — Proof in silver *FDC* (0.999) (Edition: 12,000 including coins in sets)*

4540 Britannia. Twenty pence. (1/10 oz of fine silver) R. A design of the standing figure
of Britannia baring a trident and shield, with a lion at her feet, set against the backdrop
of a globe , and with the inscription ' BRITANNIA 999 1/10 OZ FINE SILVER 2014'
(Reverse design: Jody Clark)
2014— Proof in silver *FDC* (0.999) (Edition: 3,300 including coins in sets)*

Obverse portrait by Raphael Maklouf

4300B

4300B Britannia. Fifty pence. (1/4 oz of fine silver) 10th Anniversary of Britannia issue R. The
figure of Britannia standing in a chariot drawn along the seashore by two horses, with the
word 'BRITANNIA', the inscription. '1/4 OUNCE FINE SILVER' and the date of the year.
(Reverse design: Philip Nathan).
1997 Proof *FDC* (in 1997 sets, see PSB01)* £30

* Coins marked thus were originally issued in Royal Mint sets.

Obverse portrait by Ian Rank-Broadley

                          4520   4521

4520 **Britannia. Fifty pence.** (1/4 oz of fine silver) R. The figure of Britannia standing upon a rock in the sea, her right hand grasping a trident and her left hand resting on a shield and holding an olive branch, the word 'BRITANNIA', the date of the year, and the inscription '1/4 OUNCE FINE SILVER'. (Reverse design: Philip Nathan). (See 4500)
1998 — Proof *FDC* (in 1998 set, see PSB02)* £25
2012 — Proof *FDC* (Edition: 2,600 in sets see PBS14)*

4520A **Britannia. Fifty pence.** (1/4 oz of fine silver, 0.999 fine) R. The figure of Britannia standing upon a rock in the sea, her .right hand grasping a trident and her left hand resting on a shield and holding an olive branch, with the word 'BRITANNIA', the date of the year, and the inscription' ¼ OUNCE FINE SILVER'. With the edge inscription 'SS Gairsoppa' (Reverse design: Philip Nathan)
2013
2014 (Edition: 20,000) £20

4521 **Britannia. Fifty pence.** (1/4 oz of fine silver) R. The figure of Britannia, as guardian, with a shield in her left hand and a trident in her right hand, accompanied by a lion and, against the background of a wave motif, the words '(1/4 OUNCE FINE SILVER' to the left and 'BRITANNIA' and the date of the year to the right. . (Reverse design: Philip Nathan).
2001 — Proof *FDC* (in 2001 set, see PSB03)* £25

                          4522   4524

4522 **Britannia. Fifty pence.** (1/4 oz fine silver) R. Helmeted head of Britannia with, to the left, the word 'BRITANNIA' and, to the right, the inscription '1/4 OUNCE FINE SILVER' and the date of the year, the whole being overlaid with a wave pattern. (Reverse design: Philip Nathan)
2003 — Proof *FDC*...£25

4523 **Britannia. Fifty pence.** (Previously listed as 4514) (1/4 oz of fine silver) R. Seated figure of Britannia facing to the left holding a trident with a shield at her side, with the word 'BRITANNIA', the inscription '1/4 OUNCE FINE SILVER' and the date of the year. (Reverse design: Philip Nathan). (See 4504)
2005 — Proof *FDC*...£25

4524 **Britannia. Fifty pence.** (1/4 oz of fine silver) R. Seated figure of Britannia facing right holding a trident in her right hand and a sprig of olive in the left hand with a lion at her feet with the inscription '1/4 OUNCE FINE SILVER' and the word 'BRITANNIA' and the date of the year (See 4505) (Reverse design: Christopher Le Brun)
2007 — Proof *FDC*...£25

* Coins marked thus were originally issued in Royal Mint sets.

4525　　　　　　4527　　　　　　　　　　　4529

4525　Britannia. Fifty pence. (1/4 oz of fine silver) R. A Standing figure of Britannia holding a trident with a shield at her side, the folds of her dress transforming into a wave, with the word 'BRITANNIA' and the date of the year and the inscription '1/4 OUNCE FINE SILVER' (Reverse design: John Bergdahl)
2008 — Proof *FDC** £25

4526　Britannia. Fifty pence. (1/4 oz fine silver) R. Standing figure of Britannia in horse drawn chariot. (see 4300B above)
2009 — Proof *FDC**...£30

4527　Britannia. Fifty pence. (1/4 oz fine silver) R. A design depicting a profile bust of Britannia wearing a helmet, accompanied by the name 'BRITANNIA', the inscription '1/4 OUNCE FINE SILVER' and the date '2010'. (Reverse design: Suzie Zamit)
2010 Proof *FDC* * £30

4528 Britannia. Fifty pence. (1/4 oz fine silver) R. A design depicting a seated figure of Britannia set against a background of a rippling Union Flag accompanied by the words '1/4 OUNCE FINE SILVER BRITANNIA' and the date '2011'. (Reverse design: David Mach)
2011 Proof *FDC* (Edition: 5,000 including coins in sets)....................................£30

4529　Britannia. Fifty pence. (1/4 oz of fine silver).R. . Seated figure of Britannia holding a trident with a shield at her side and an owl upon her knee with the word 'BRITANNIA' and the date of the year above and the inscription '1/4 OUNCE FINE SILVER' below the figure of Britannia. (Reverse design: Robert Hunt)
2013 — Proof in silver *FDC* (0.999) (Edition: 4,500 including coins in sets)*

4530　Britannia. Fifty pence. (1/4 oz of fine silver) R. A design of the standing figure of Britannia baring a trident and shield, with a lion at her feet, set against the backdrop of a globe, and with the inscription 'BRITANNIA 999 1/4 OZ FINE SILVER 2014' (Reverse design: Jody Clark)
2014 — Proof in silver *FDC* (0.999) (Edition: 2,300 including coins in sets)*

Obverse portrait by Raphael Maklouf

4300A

4300ABritannia. One pound. (1/2 oz of fine silver) 10th Anniversary of Britannia issue. R. The figure of Britannia standing in a chariot drawn along the seashore by two horses, with the word 'BRITANNIA', the inscription. '1/2 OUNCE FINE SILVER' and the date of the year. (Reverse design: Philip Nathan).
1997 Proof *FDC** £40

* Coins marked thus were originally issued in Royal Mint sets.

Obverse portrait by Ian Rank-Broadley

4510

4510 Britannia. One pound. (1/2 oz of fine silver) R. The figure of Britannia standing upon a
rock in the sea, her right hand grasping a trident and her left hand resting on a shield and
holding an olive branch, with the word 'BRITANNIA', the date of the year, and the
inscription '1/2 OUNCE FINE SILVER' (Reverse design: Philip Nathan).
1998 — Proof *FDC** £40
2012 — Proof *FDC* (Edition: 4,620 in sets see PBS14 and PBS15)*
4510A 2007 Proof with satin finish on reverse (see 2007 set, PBS09) * £40

4511   4512   4514

4511 Britannia. One pound. (1/2oz of fine silver) R The figure of Britannia, as guardian,
with a shield in her left hand and a trident in her right hand, accompanied by a lion
and, against the background of a wave motif, the words '1/2 OUNCE FINE SILVER'
to the left and 'BRITANNIA' and the date of the year to the right. (Reverse design:
Philip Nathan).
2001 — Proof *FDC** £40
2012 — Proof *FDC* (Edition: 2,012 in sets see PBS15)*
4511A 2007 Proof with satin finish on reverse (see 2007 set, PBS09) * £40
4512 Britannia. One pound. (1/2 oz fine silver) R. Helmeted head of Britannia with, to the
left, the word 'BRITANNIA' and, to the right, the inscription '1/2 OUNCE FINE
SILVER' and the date of the year, the whole being overlaid with a wave pattern.
(Reverse design: Philip Nathan)
2003 — Proof *FDC** £40
2012 — Proof *FDC* (Edition: 2,012 in sets see PBS15)*
4512A 2007 Proof with satin finish on reverse (see 2007 set, PBS09) * £40
4513 Britannia. One pound. (1/2 oz of fine silver) R. Seated figure of Britannia facing to
the left holding a trident with a shield at her side, with the word 'BRITANNIA', the
inscription '1/2 OUNCE FINE SILVER' and the date of the year. (Reverse design:
Philip Nathan). (See 4504)
2005 — Proof *FDC** £40
2012 — Proof *FDC* (Edition: 2,012 in sets see PBS15)*
4513A 2007 Proof with satin finish on reverse (see 2007 set, PBS09) * £40

* *Coins marked thus were originally issued in Royal Mint sets.*

4514 Britannia. One pound. (1/2 oz of fine silver) R. Seated figure of Britannia facing right holding a trident in her right hand and a sprig of olive in the left hand with a lion at her feet with the inscription '1/2 OUNCE FINE SILVER' and the word 'BRITANNIA' and the date of the year. (Reverse design: Christopher Le Brun)
2007 Proof *FDC* * £40
2012 — Proof *FDC* (Edition: 2,012 in sets see PBS15)*
4514A 2007 Proof with satin finish on reverse (see 2007 set, PBS09) * £40
4515 Britannia. One pound. (1/2 oz of fine silver) R. Standing figure of Britannia in horse drawn chariot. (See 4300A)
2007 Proof with satin finish on reverse (see 2007 set, PBS09) * £40

4516   4517

4516 Britannia. One pound. (1/2 oz of fine silver) R. A Standing figure of Britannia holding a trident with a shield at her side, the folds of her dress transforming into a wave, with the word 'BRITANNIA' and the date of the year and the inscription '1/2 OUNCE FINE SILVER' (Reverse design: John Bergdahl)
2008 Proof *FDC* * £40
2012 — Proof *FDC* (Edition: 2,012 in sets see PBS15)*
4517 Britannia. One pound. (1/2 oz fine silver) R. Standing figure of Britannia in horse drawn chariot. (Reverse design: Philip Nathan) (See 4300A above)
2009 — Proof *FDC* * £40
2012 — Proof *FDC* (Edition: 2,012 in sets see PBS15)*

4518   4519

4518 Britannia. One pound. (1/2 oz fine silver) R. A design depicting a profile bust of Britannia wearing a helmet, accompanied by the name 'BRITANNIA', the inscription '1/2 OUNCE FINE SILVER' and the date '2010'. (Reverse design: Suzie Zamit)
2010 Proof *FDC* * £40
2012 — Proof *FDC* (Edition: 2,012 in sets see PBS15)*
4519 Britannia. One pound. (1/2 oz fine silver) R. A design depicting a seated figure of Britannia set against a background of a rippling Union Flag accompanied by the words '1/2 OUNCE FINE SILVER BRITANNIA' and the date '2011'. (Reverse design: David Mach)
2011 Proof *FDC* (Edition: 5,000 including coins in sets) £40
2012 — Proof *FDC* (Edition: 2,012 in sets see PBS15)*

* *Coins marked thus were originally issued in Royal Mint sets.*

4700

4700 Britannia. One pound. (1/2 oz of fine silver) R. Seated figure of Britannia holding
a trident with a shield at her side and an owl upon her knee with the word
'BRITANNIA' and the date of the year above and the inscription '1/2 OUNCE FINE
SILVER' below the figure of Britannia. (Reverse design: Robert Hunt)
2013 — Proof in silver *FDC* (0.999) (Edition: 4,500 including coins in sets)*

4701 Britannia. One pound. (1/2 oz of fine silver) R. A design of the standing figure of
Britannia baring a trident and shield, with a lion at her feet, set against the backdrop
of a globe , and with the inscription ' BRITANNIA 999 1/2 OZ FINE SILVER 2014'
(Reverse design: Jody Clark)
2014 — Proof in silver *FDC* (0.999) (Edition: 2,300 including coins in sets)*

Obverse portrait by Raphael Maklouf

4300

4300 Britannia. Two pounds. (1 oz fine silver) 10th Anniversary of Britannia issue R. The
figure of Britannia standing in a chariot drawn along the seashore by two horses, with the
word 'BRITANNIA', the inscription. 'ONE OUNCE FINE SILVER' and the date of the
year. (Reverse design: Philip Nathan)
1997 Proof *FDC* (Issued: 4,173) £120

* Coins marked thus were originally issued in Royal Mint sets.

Obverse portrait by Ian Rank-Broadley

4500

4500 **Britannia. Two pounds.** (1 oz of fine silver) R. The figure of Britannia standing upon a
rock in the sea, her right hand grasping a trident and her left hand resting on a shield and
holding an olive branch, with the word 'BRITANNIA', the date of the year, and the
inscription' ONE OUNCE FINE SILVER'. (Reverse design: Philip Nathan)

1998 (Issued: 88,909).......................£40	2006 (Edition 100,000).............................£40
— Proof *FDC* (Issued: 2,168)......£80	— Proof *FDC* (Issued: 2,529) £65
2000 (Issued: 81,301).......................£40	2012 (Edition 100,000).............................£58
2002 (Issued: 36,543).......................£40	— Proof *FDC* (Edition 5,550 including coins
2004 (Edition: 100,000) £40	in sets) £93
— Proof *FDC* (Issued: 2,174)......£65	

4500A Britannia. Two pounds. (1 oz of fine silver) R. Standing figure of Britannia
2006 - Proof *FDC** with selected gold plating of obverse and reverse (See PBS07).......£70
4500B Britannia. Two pounds. (1 oz. of fine silver – 0.999) R. Reverse as 4500 above.
2013
4500C Britannia. Two pounds. (1 oz. of fine silver – 0.999) R. As 4500 above but with revised
inscription 'BRITANNIA 2014 1 oz. 999 FINE SILVER'
2014

—   (Edition: 10,000) £58
4500D Britannia. Two pounds. (Previously listed as 4500B). (1 oz. of fine silver – 0.999)
2013

—   As 4500 above but with edge decoration of snake design symbolising the Year of the Snake.
4500E Britannia. Two pounds. (1 oz. of fine silver – 0.999)
2014

—   As 4500 above but with edge decoration of horse design symbolising Year of the Horse
4500F Two pounds. Error obverse – known as a Mule. The obverse design of The Queen
used for the Year of the Horse £2 Silver coin was paired with the reverse design of the
Britannia £2 silver coin.
2014

* Coins marked thus were originally issued in Royal Mint sets.

4501   4502

4501 Britannia. Two pounds. (1oz fine silver) R. Standing figure of Britannia in horse drawn
chariot.(Reverse design: Philip Nathan)
1999 (Issued: 69,394)...£40
2009 (Issued: 100,000)..£40
— Proof *FDC* (Edition: 12,000 including coins in sets)...£65
4501A Britannia. Two pounds. (1 oz of fine silver) R. Standing figure of Britannia in horse
drawn chariot
2006 — Proof *FDC** with selected gold plating of obverse and reverse (See PBS07)....£70
4502 Britannia. Two pounds. (1 oz of fine silver) R. The figure of Britannia, as guardian, with
a shield in her left hand and a trident in her right hand, accompanied by a lion and, against
the background of a wave motif, the words 'ONE OUNCE FINE SILVER' to the left and
'BRITANNIA' and the date of the year to the right. (Reverse design: Philip Nathan)
2001 (Issued: 44,816)...£40
— Proof *FDC* (Issued: 3,047)...£60
4502A Britannia. Two pounds. (1 oz of fine silver) R. Helmeted figure of Britannia holding a
trident and a shield with a lion in the background
2006 — Proof *FDC** with selected gold plating of obverse and reverse (See PBS07)....£70

* *Coins marked thus were originally issued in Royal Mint sets.*

4503   4504

4503 Britannia. Two pounds. (1oz fine silver) R. Helmeted head of Britannia with, to the left,
the word 'BRITANNIA' and, to the right, the inscription 'ONE OUNCE FINE SILVER'
and the date of the year, ...the whole being overlaid with a wave pattern. (Reverse design:
Philip Nathan)
2003 (Issued: 73,271)..£40
—   Proof *FDC* (Issued: 2,016)..£65
4503A Britannia. Two pounds. (1oz fine silver) R. Helmeted figure of Britannia with stylised waves
2006 — Proof *FDC** with selected gold plating of obverse and reverse (See PBS07)....£70
4504 Britannia. Two pounds. (1 oz of fine silver) R. Seated figure of Britannia facing to the
left holding a trident with a shield at her side, with the word 'BRITANNIA', the inscription
'ONE OUNCE FINE SILVER' and the date of the year. (Reverse design: Philip Nathan)
2005 (Edition: 100,000) £40
—   Proof *FDC* (Issued: 1,539)..£65
4504A Britannia. Two pounds. (1 oz of fine silver) R. Seated figure of Britannia facing left
2006 — Proof *FDC** with selected gold plating of obverse and reverse (See PBS07)....£70

4505   4506

4505 Britannia. Two pounds. (1 oz of fine silver) R. Seated figure of Britannia facing right
holding a trident in her right hand and a sprig of olive in the left hand with a lion at her feet
with the inscription 'ONE OUNCE FINE SILVER' and the word 'BRITANNIA' and the
date of the year (See 4505) (Reverse design: Christopher Le Brun)
2007 (Edition: 100,000) £40
—   Proof *FDC* (Issued: 5,157 ....£65
4506 Britannia. Two pounds. (1 oz of fine silver) R. A Standing figure of Britannia holding a
trident with a shield at her side, the folds of her dress transforming into a wave, with the word
'BRITANNIA' and the date of the year and the inscription 'ONE OUNCE FINE SILVER'
(Reverse design: John Bergdahl)
2008 (Edition: 100,000) £40
—   Proof *FDC* (Edition: 2,500) £65

* *Coins marked thus were originally issued in Royal Mint sets.*

4507   4508

4507 **Britannia. Two pounds.** (1 oz fine silver) R. A design depicting a profile bust of
Britannia wearing a helmet, accompanied by the name 'BRITANNIA', the inscription
'ONE OUNCE FINE SILVER' and the date '2010'. (Reverse design: Suzie Zamit)
2010 (Edition: 100,000) £40
  —   Proof *FDC* (Edition: 8,000 including coins in sets)..£65

4508 **Britannia. Two pounds.** (1 oz fine silver) R. A design depicting a seated figure of Britannia
set against a background of a rippling Union Flag accompanied by the words 'ONE OUNCE
FINE SILVER BRITANNIA' and the date '2011'. (Reverse design: David Mach)
2011 (Edition: 500,000)...£58
  —   Proof *FDC* (Edition: 10,000) £90

4509

4509 **Britannia. Two pounds.** (1 oz of fine silver) R. Seated figure of Britannia holding a
trident with a shield at her side and an owl upon her knee with the word 'BRITANNIA'
and the date of the year above and the inscription 'ONE OUNCE FINE SILVER' below
the figure of Britannia. (Reverse design: Robert Hunt)
2013 — Proof in silver *FDC* (0.999) (Edition: 8,500 including coins in sets) £93

4540 **Britannia. Two pounds.** (1 oz of fine silver) R. A design of the standing figure of
Britannia baring a trident and shield, with a lion at her feet, set against the backdrop
of a globe, and with the inscription 'BRITANNIA 999 ONE OZ FINE SILVER 2014'
(Reverse design: Jody Clark)
2014 — Proof in silver *FDC* (0.999) (Edition: 5,300 including coins in sets) £93

4810

4810 Britannia. Ten pounds. (5 oz of fine silver).R. . Seated figure of Britannia holding a
       trident with a shield at her side and an owl upon her knee with the word 'BRITANNIA'
       and the date of the year above and the inscription 'FIVE OUNCES FINE SILVER'
       below the figure of Britannia. (Reverse design: Robert Hunt)
       2013 — Proof in silver FDC (0.999) (Edition: 4,650) £450
       Illustration shown at a reduced size - actual coin diameter 63mm

4810

4811 Britannia. Ten pounds. (5 oz. of fine silver) R. A design of the standing figure of
       Britannia baring a trident and shield, with a lion at her feet, set against the backdrop
       of a globe, and with the inscription 'BRITANNIA 999.9 FIVE OZ FINE SILVER 2014'
       (Reverse design: Jody Clark)
       2014 — Proof in silver *FDC* (0.999) (Edition: 1,350) £395
       Illustration shown at a reduced size - actual coin diameter 63mm
4820 Britannia. Fifty pounds. (1 kilo of fine silver). R. A design of the figure of Britannia
       on a textured background standing upon a rock in the sea, her right hand grasping a
       trident and her left hand on a shield and holding an olive branch, with the inscription
       'BRITANNIA' (and the date of the year) 1KILO OF 999 FINE SILVER' (Original
       reverse design: Philip Nathan)
       2014

* Coins marked thus were originally issued in Royal Mint sets.

BRITANNIA GOLD

Obverse portrait by Ian Rank-Broadley

4740

4740 Britannia. 50 pence. (1/40 oz. of fine gold) R. A design of the standing figure of Britannia baring a trident and shield, with a lion at her feet, set against the backdrop of a globe, and with the inscription 'BRITANNIA 999.9 1/40 OZ FINE GOLD 2014' (Reverse design: Jody Clark)

2014 — Proof in gold *FDC* (0.9999) (Edition: 10,000 including coins in sets)*
Illustration shown larger than actual coin diameter of 8mm

4775 Britannia. One pound. (1/20 oz of fine gold) R. Seated figure of Britannia holding a trident with a shield at her side and an owl upon her knee with the word 'BRITANNIA' and the date of the year above and the inscription '1/20 OUNCE FINE GOLD' below the figure of Britannia. (Reverse design: Robert Hunt)

2013 — Proof in gold *FDC* (0.9999) (Edition: 5,750 including coins in sets)

4776 Britannia. One pound. (1/20 oz of fine gold) R. A design of the standing figure of Britannia baring a trident and shield, with a lion at her feet, set against the backdrop of a globe , and with the inscription ' BRITANNIA 999.9 1/20 OZ FINE GOLD 2014' (Reverse design: Jody Clark)

2014 — Proof in gold *FDC* (0.9999) (Edition: 1,550 including coins in sets)* £100

Obverse portrait by Raphael Maklouf

4296

4296 Britannia. Ten pounds. (1/10oz of fine gold alloyed with copper). R. The figure of Britannia standing upon a rock in the sea, her right hand grasping a trident and her left hand resting on a shield and holding an olive branch, with the inscription '1/10 OUNCE FINE GOLD BRITANNIA' and the year of the date. (Reverse design: Philip Nathan)

1987............................ £130		1989 .... £130	
— Proof *FDC* (Issued: 3,500).... £150		— Proof *FDC* (Issued: 1,609) £150	
1988............................ £130			
— Proof *FDC* (Issued: 2,694).... £150			

4297 Britannia. Ten pounds. (1/10oz of fine gold alloyed with silver). R. Britannia standing.

1990............................ £130		1994 .... £130	
— Proof *FDC* (Issued: 1,571).... £150		— Proof *FDC* (Issued: 994) £150	
1991............................ £130		1995 .... £130	
— Proof *FDC* (Issued: 954)....... £150		— Proof *FDC* (Issued: 1,500) £150	
1992............................ £130		1996 .... £130	
— Proof *FDC* (Issued: 1,000).... £150		— Proof *FDC* (Issued: 2,379) £150	
1993............................ £130			
— Proof *FDC* (Issued: 997)....... £150			

* Coins marked thus were originally issued in Royal Mint sets.
NB. The spot price of gold at the time of going to press was £720 per oz.

4298

4298 Britannia. Ten pounds. (1/10 oz fine gold, alloyed with silver) 10th Anniversary of
Britannia issue. R. The figure of Britannia standing in a chariot drawn along the seashore
by two horses, with the word 'BRITANNIA', .the inscription '1/10 OUNCE FINE GOLD'
and the date of the year. (Reverse design: Philip Nathan)
1997 Proof *FDC* (Issued: 1,821) £180

Obverse portrait by Ian Rank-Broadley

4480   4481   4482   4483

4480 Britannia. Ten pounds. (1/10 oz fine gold alloyed with silver) R. The figure of Britannia
standing upon a rock in the sea, Her right hand grasping a trident and her left hand resting
on a shield and holding an olive branch, with the word 'BRITANNIA', the date of the year,
and the inscription '1/10 OUNCE FINE GOLD'. (Reverse design: Philip Nathan)

1998 Proof *FDC* (Issued: 392)...... £150	2002 Proof *FDC* (Issued: 1,500) £150
1999..£130	2004..£130
1999 Proof *FDC* (Issued: 1,058)... £150	2004 Proof *FDC* (Issued: 929) £150
2000..£130	2006 Proof *FDC* (issued: 700)..................£150
2000 Proof *FDC* (Issued: 659)...... £150	2012 ....£150
2002..£130	2012 Proof *FDC* (Edition: 2,500)............£225

4481 Britannia. Ten pounds. (1/10 oz fine gold alloyed with silver) R. The figure of Britannia, as
guardian, with a shield in her left hand and a trident in her right hand, accompanied by a lion
and, against the background of a wave motif, and the words '1/10 OUNCE FINE GOLD' to the
left and 'BRITANNIA' and the date of the year to the right. (Reverse design: Philip Nathan)
2001 .... £130   2001 Proof *FDC* (Issued: 1,557) £150

4482 Britannia. Ten pounds. (1/10 oz fine gold alloyed with silver) R. . Helmeted head of Britannia
with, to the left, the word 'BRITANNIA' and, to the right, the inscription '1/10 OUNCE FINE
GOLD' and the date of the year, the whole being overlaid with a wave pattern. (Reverse design:
Philip Nathan)
2003.. £130   2003 Proof *FDC* (Issued: 1,382) £150

4483 Britannia. Ten pounds. (1/10 oz fine gold alloyed with silver) R. Seated figure of Britannia
facing to the left holding a trident with a shield at her side, with the word 'BRITANNIA', the
inscription '1/10 OUNCE FINE GOLD' and the date of the year. (Reverse design: Philip Nathan)
2005 Proof *FDC* (issued: 1,225) £150

* Coins marked thus were originally issued in Royal Mint sets.
NB. The spot price of gold at the time of going to press was £720 per oz.

4484	4485	4486	4487

4484 **Britannia. Ten pounds.** (1/10 oz fine gold alloyed with silver) R. Seated figure of
Britannia facing right holding a trident in her right hand and a sprig of olive in the left
hand with a lion at her feet with the inscription '1/10 OUNCE FINE GOLD' and the word
'BRITANNIA' and the date of the year. (Reverse design: Christopher Le Brun)
2007... £130   2007 Proof *FDC* (Issued: 893) £150

4484A(1/10 oz platinum)
2007 Proof *FDC* (Issued: 691) £225

4485 **Britannia. Ten pounds.** (1/10 oz fine gold alloyed with silver) R. A Standing figure of
Britannia holding a trident with a shield at her side, the folds of her dress transforming
into a wave, with the word 'BRITANNIA' and the date of the year and the inscription '1/10
OUNCE FINE GOLD' (Reverse design: John Bergdahl)
2008 Proof *FDC* (Issued: 748 plus coins issued in sets, see PBS30) £150

4485A(1/10 oz platinum)
2008 Proof *FDC* (Issued: 268 plus coins issued in sets, see PPBCS2) £225

4486 **Britannia. Ten pounds.** (1/10 oz fine gold alloyed with silver) R. Standing figure of
Britannia in horse drawn chariot.
2009... £130   2009 Proof *FDC* (Edition: 750)...............£160

4487 **Britannia. Ten pounds.** (1/10 oz fine gold alloyed with silver) R. A design depicting a
profile bust of Britannia wearing a helmet, accompanied by the name 'BRITANNIA', the
inscription '1/10 OUNCE FINE GOLD' and the date '2010'. (Reverse design: Suzie Zamit)
2010 Proof *FDC* (Edition: 3,000 including coins in sets)...£160

4488 **Britannia. Ten pounds.** (1/10 oz fine gold alloyed with silver) R. A design depicting a
seated figure of Britannia set against a background of a rippling Union Flag accompanied by
the words '1/10 OUNCE FINE GOLD BRITANNIA, and the date '2011'. (Reverse design:
David Mach)
2011 Proof *FDC* (Edition: 8,000 including coins in sets) £225

4489

4489 **Britannia. Ten pounds.** (1/10 oz of fine gold) R. Seated figure of Britannia holding a trident
with a shield at her side and an owl upon her knee with the word 'BRITANNIA' and the
date of the year above and the inscription '1/10 OUNCE FINE GOLD' below the figure of
Britannia. (Reverse design: Robert Hunt)
2013 — Proof in gold *FDC* (0.9999) (Edition: 1,125 including coins in sets)*

4490 **Britannia. Ten pounds.** (1/10 oz of fine gold) R. A design of the standing figure of Britannia
baring a trident and shield, with a lion at her feet, set against the backdrop of a globe, and with
the inscription 'BRITANNIA 999.9 1/10 OZ FINE GOLD 2014' (Reverse design: Jody Clark)
2014 — Proof in gold *FDC* (0.9999) (Edition: 650 including coins in sets)*

* Coins marked thus were originally issued in Royal Mint sets.
NB. The spot price of gold at the time of going to press was £720 per oz.

Obverse portrait by Raphael Maklouf

4291

4291 Britannia. Twenty five pounds. (1/4oz of fine gold alloyed with copper). R. The figure of Britannia standing upon a rock in the sea, her right hand grasping a trident and her left hand resting on a shield and holding an olive branch, with the inscription '1/4 OUNCE FINE GOLD BRITANNIA' and the year of the date. (Reverse design: Philip Nathan)

1987	£325	1989	£325
— Proof *FDC* (Issued: 3,500)	£350	— Proof *FDC* (see PBS05)*	£350
1988	£325		
— Proof *FDC* (see PBS03)*	£350		

4292 Britannia. Twenty five pounds. (1/4oz of fine gold alloyed with silver). R. Britannia standing.

1990	£325	1994	£325
— Proof *FDC* (see PBS07)*	£350	— Proof *FDC* (see PBS11)*	£350
1991	£325	1995	£325
— Proof *FDC* (see PBS08)*	£350	— Proof *FDC* (see PBS12)*	£350
1992	£325	1996	£325
— Proof *FDC* (see PBS09)*	£350	— Proof *FDC* (see PBS13	£350
1993	£325		
— Proof *FDC* (see PBS10)*	£350		

4293

4293 Britannia. Twenty five pounds. (1/4 oz fine gold, alloyed with silver) 10th Anniversary of Britannia issue. R. The figure of Britannia standing in a chariot drawn along the seashore by two horses, with the word 'BRITANNIA', ..the inscription. '1/4 OUNCE FINE GOLD' and the date of the year. (Reverse design: Philip Nathan)

1997 Proof *FDC* (Issued: 923) £350

* Coins marked thus were originally issued in Royal Mint sets.

NB. The spot price of gold at the time of going to press was £720 per oz.

Obverse portrait by Ian Rank-Broadley

4470

4470 **Britannia. Twenty five pounds.** (1/4 oz fine gold alloyed with silver) R. The figure of
Britannia standing upon a rock in the sea, her right hand grasping a trident and her left hand
resting on a shield and holding an olive branch, with the word 'BRITANNIA', the date of the
year, and the inscription' 1/4 OUNCE FINE GOLD'. (Reverse design: Philip Nathan)

1998 Proof *FDC* (Issued: 560)...... £350	2002 Proof *FDC* (Issued: 750) £350
1999... £325	2004 Proof *FDC* (Issued: 750) £350
1999 Proof *FDC* (Issued: 1,000)... £350	2006 Proof *FDC* (Edition: 1,000)............£350
2000... £325	2012 Proof *FDC* (Edition: 1,750)............£500
2000 Proof *FDC* (Issued: 500)...... £350	

4471   4472   4475

4471 **Britannia. Twenty five pounds.** (1/4 oz fine gold alloyed with silver) R. The figure of
Britannia, as guardian, with a shield in her left hand and a trident in her right hand,
accompanied by a lion and, against the background of a wave motif, the words '1/4
OUNCE FINE GOLD' to the left and 'BRITANNIA' and the date of the year to the right.
(Reverse design: Philip Nathan)

2001 .... £325	2006 Proof *FDC* (see PBS28)* £350
2001 Proof *FDC* (Issued: 500)...... £350	

4472 **Britannia. Twenty five pounds.** (1/4 oz fine gold alloyed with silver) R. Helmeted head
of Britannia with, to the left, the word 'BRITANNIA' and, to the right, the inscription '1/4
OUNCE FINE GOLD' and the date of the year, the whole being overlaid with a wave
pattern. (Reverse design: Philip Nathan)

2003 Proof *FDC* (Issued: 609)...... £325	2006 Proof *FDC* (see PBS28)* £350

4473 **Britannia. Twenty five pounds.** (1/4 oz fine gold alloyed with silver) R. Seated figure
of Britannia facing to the left holding a trident with a shield at her side, with the word
'BRITANNIA', the inscription '1/4 OUNCE FINE GOLD' and the date of the year.
(Reverse design: Philip Nathan)

2005 Proof *FDC* (Issued: 750) £325	2006 Proof *FDC* (seePBS28)* £350

4474 **Britannia. Twenty five pounds.** (1/4 oz fine gold alloyed with silver) R. Standing figure
of Britannia in horse drawn chariot. (See 4293)

2006 Proof *FDC* (see PBS28)* £325	2009 Proof *FDC* (Edition: 1,000) £350

4475 **Britannia. Twenty five pounds.** (Previously listed as 4474) (1/4 oz fine gold alloyed
with silver) R. Seated figure of Britannia facing right holding a trident in her right
hand and a sprig of olive in the left hand with a lion at her feet with the inscription '1/4
OUNCE FINE GOLD' and the word 'BRITANNIA' and the date of the year. (Reverse
design: Christopher Le Brun)

2007..£325	2007 Proof *FDC* (Issued: 1,000) £350

* Coins marked thus were originally issued in Royal Mint sets.
NB. The spot price of gold at the time of going to press was £720 per oz.

4475A (1/4 oz platinum)
   2007 Proof *FDC* (Issued: 210) £450

4476   4477

4476 Britannia. Twenty five pounds. (1/4 oz fine gold alloyed with silver) R. A Standing
       figure of Britannia holding a trident with a shield at her side, the folds of her dress
       transforming into a wave, with the word 'BRITANNIA' and the date of the year and the
       inscription '1/4 OUNCE FINE GOLD' (Reverse design: John Bergdahl)
       2008 Proof *FDC* (Edition: 1,000) £350
4476A (1/4 oz platinum)
   2008 Proof *FDC* (Edition: 500) £450
4477 Britannia. Twenty five pounds. (1/4 oz fine gold alloyed with silver) R. A design
       depicting a profile bust of Britannia wearing a helmet, accompanied by the name
       'BRITANNIA', the inscription '1/4 OUNCE FINE GOLD' and the date '2010'. (Reverse
       design: Suzie Zamit)
       2010 Proof *FDC* (Edition: 3,000 including coins in sets)...£350
4478 Britannia. Twenty Five pounds. (1/4 oz fine gold alloyed with silver) R. A design
       depicting a seated figure of Britannia set against a background of a rippling Union Flag
       accompanied by the words ' 1/4 OUNCE FINE GOLD BRITANNIA, and the date
       '2011'. (Reverse design: David Mach)
       2011 Proof *FDC* (Edition: 7,000 including coins in sets) £500
4479 Britannia. Twenty five pounds. (1/4 oz of fine gold) R. Seated figure of Britannia
       holding a trident with a shield at her side and an owl upon her knee with the word
       'BRITANNIA' and the date of the year above and the inscription '1/4 OUNCE FINE
       GOLD' below the figure of Britannia. (Reverse design: Robert Hunt)
       2013 — Proof in gold *FDC* (0.9999) (Edition: 875 including coins in sets)*

4480

4480 Britannia. Twenty five pounds. (1/4 oz of fine gold) R. A design of the standing figure
       of Britannia baring a trident and shield, with a lion at her feet, set against the backdrop
       of a globe , and with the inscription ' BRITANNIA 999.9 1/4 OZ FINE GOLD 2014'
       (Reverse design: Jody Clark)...
       2014 — Proof in gold *FDC* (0.9999) (Edition: 650 including coins in sets)*

* Coins marked thus were originally issued in Royal Mint sets.
NB. The spot price of gold at the time of going to press was £720 per oz.

Obverse portrait by Raphael Maklouf

4288

4286 Britannia. Fifty pounds. (1/2oz of fine gold alloyed with copper). R. The figure of
Britannia standing upon a rock in the sea, her right hand grasping a trident and her left
hand resting on a shield and holding an olive branch, with the inscription '1/2 OUNCE
FINE GOLD BRITANNIA' and the year of the date. (Reverse design: Philip Nathan)

1987... £650	1989 ....£650
— Proof *FDC* (Issued: 2,486).... £700	— Proof *FDC* (see PBS05)* £700
1988... £650	
— Proof *FDC* (see PBS03)* £700	

4288

4287 Britannia. Fifty pounds. (1/2oz of fine gold, alloyed with Silver). R. Britannia standing.

1990... £650	1994 ....£650
— Proof *FDC* (see PBS07)* £700	— Proof *FDC* (see PBS11)*.................£700
1991... £650	1995 ....£650
— Proof *FDC* (see PBS08)* £700	— Proof *FDC* (see PBS12)* £700
1992... £650	1996 ....£650
— Proof *FDC* (see PBS09)* £700	— Proof *FDC* (see PBS13)* £700
1993... £650	
— Proof *FDC* (see PBS10)* £700	

4288 Britannia. Fifty pounds. (1/2 oz fine gold, alloyed with silver) 10th Anniversary of
Britannia issue. R.The figure of Britannia standing in a chariot drawn along the seashore
by two horses, with the word 'BRITANNIA', the inscription. '1/2 FINE GOLD' and the
date of the year. (Reverse design: Philip Nathan)

1997 Proof *FDC* (see PBS14)* £700

* Coins marked thus were originally issued in Royal Mint sets.
NB. The spot price of gold at the time of going to press was £720 per oz.

Obverse portrait by Ian Rank-Broadley

4460	4461

4460 **Britannia. Fifty pounds.** (1/2 oz fine gold alloyed with silver). R. The figure of Britannia standing upon a rock in the sea, her right hand grasping a trident and her left hand resting on a shield and holding an olive branch, with the word 'BRITANNIA', the date of the year, and the inscription' 1/2 OUNCE FINE GOLD'. (Reverse design: Philip Nathan)

1998 Proof *FDC* (see PBS15)* £700	2002 Proof *FDC* (see PBS19)* £700
1999 ....£650	2004 Proof *FDC* (see PBS23)* £700
1999 Proof *FDC* (see PBS16)* £700	2006 Proof *FDC* (see PBS27)* £700
2000 ....£650	2012 Proof *FDC* (Edition: 1,000) £700
— Proof *FDC* (see PBS17)* £700	

4461 **Britannia. Fifty pounds.** (1/2 oz fine gold alloyed with silver). R. The figure of Britannia, as guardian, with a shield in her left hand and a trident in her right hand, accompanied by a lion and, against the background of a wave motif, the words '1/2 OUNCE FINE GOLD' to the left and 'BRITANNIA' and the date of the year to the right. (Reverse design: Philip Nathan)

2001 ....£650	2001 Proof *FDC* (see PBS18)* £700

4463	4464	4465

4462 **Britannia. Fifty pounds.** (1/2 oz fine gold alloyed with silver) R. Helmeted head of Britannia with, to the left, the word 'BRITANNIA' and, to the right, the inscription '1/2 OUNCE FINE GOLD' and the date of the year, ...the whole being overlaid with a wave pattern. (Reverse design: Philip Nathan)

2003 ....£650	2003 Proof *FDC* (see PBS20)* £700

4463 **Britannia. Fifty pounds.** (1/2 oz fine gold alloyed with silver) R. Seated figure of Britannia facing to the left holding a trident with a shield at her side, with the word 'BRITANNIA', the inscription '1/2 OUNCE FINE GOLD' and the date of the year. (Reverse design: Philip Nathan)

2005 Proof *FDC* * £700

4464 **Britannia. Fifty pounds.** (1/2 oz fine gold alloyed with silver) R. Seated figure of Britannia facing right holding a trident in her right hand and a sprig of olive in the left hand with a lion at her feet with the inscription '1/2 OUNCE FINE GOLD' and the word 'BRITANNIA' and the date of the year (See 4505) (Reverse design: Christopher Le Brun)

2007 ....£650	2007 Proof *FDC* (see PBS29)* £700

4464A (½ oz platinum)

2007 Proof *FDC* * (see 2007 set, PPBCS1)..£800

* Coins marked thus were originally issued in Royal Mint sets.
NB. The spot price of gold at the time of going to press was £720 per oz.

4466   4467

4465   **Britannia. Fifty pounds.** (1/2 oz fine gold alloyed with silver) R. A Standing figure of
Britannia holding a trident with a shield at her side, the folds of her dress transforming
into a wave, with the word 'BRITANNIA' and the date of the year and the inscription '1/2
OUNCE FINE GOLD' (Reverse design: John Bergdahl)
2008 Proof *FDC* * £700

4465A (1/2 oz platinum)
2008 Proof *FDC* (see PPBCS2)* £800

4466   **Britannia. Fifty pounds.** (1/2oz fine gold alloyed with silver) R.Standing figure of
Britannia in horse drawn chariot.(see 4288 above)
2009 .... £650   2009 Proof *FDC* (see PBS31)* £700

4467   **Britannia. Fifty pounds.** (1/2 oz fine gold alloyed with silver) R. A design depicting a
profile bust of Britannia wearing a helmet, accompanied by the name 'BRITANNIA', the
inscription '1/2 OUNCE FINE GOLD' and the date '2010' (Reverse design: Suzie Zamit)
2010 Proof *FDC* (Edition: 1,750 in sets)* £700

4468   **Britannia. Fifty pounds.** (1/2 oz fine gold alloyed with silver) R. A design depicting a
seated figure of Britannia set against a background of a rippling Union Flag accompanied
by the words ' 1/2 OUNCE FINE GOLD BRITANNIA, and the date '2011'. (Reverse
design: David Mach)
2011 Proof *FDC* (Edition: 2,000 including coins in sets)* £700

4469

4469 Britannia. **Fifty pounds.** (1/2 oz of fine gold) R. Seated figure of Britannia holding a trident
with a shield at her side and an owl upon her knee with the word 'BRITANNIA' and the and
the inscription '1/2 OUNCE FINE GOLD' and the date '2013' below the figure of Britannia.
(Reverse design: Robert Hunt)
2013 — Proof in gold *FDC* (0.9999) (Edition: 525 including coins in sets)*

4470   **Britannia. Fifty pounds.** (1/2 oz of fine gold)..R. A design of the standing figure of
Britannia baring a trident and shield, with a lion at her feet, set against the backdrop of a
globe, and with the inscription 'BRITANNIA 999.9 1/2 OZ FINE GOLD 2014'. (Reverse
design: Jody Clark)
2014 — Proof in gold *FDC* (0.9999) (Edition: 500 including coins in sets)*

* Coins marked thus were originally issued in Royal Mint sets.
NB. The spot price of gold at the time of going to press was £720 per oz.

Obverse portrait by Raphael Maklouf

4281

4281   Britannia. One hundred pounds. (1oz of fine gold alloyed with copper) R. The figure
of Britannia standing upon a rock in the sea, her right hand grasping a trident and her left
hand resting on a shield and holding an olive branch, with the inscription ...'ONE OUNCE
FINE GOLD BRITANNIA' and the year of the date. (Reverse design: Philip Nathan)

1987... £1300		1989 .... £1300
— Proof *FDC* (Issued: 2,485).. £1350		— Proof *FDC* (Issued: 338) £1350
1988... £1300		
— Proof *FDC* (Issued: 626)..... £1350		

4282   Britannia. One hundred pounds. (1oz of fine gold alloyed with silver) R. Britannia standing.

1990... £1300	1994 .... £1300
— Proof *FDC* (Issued: 262)**. £1350	— Proof *FDC* (see PBS11)*...............£1350
1991... £1300	1995 .... £1300
— Proof *FDC* (Issued: 143)**. £1350	— Proof *FDC* (see PBS12)* £1350
1992... £1300	1996 .... £1300
— Proof *FDC* (see PBS09)* £1350	— Proof *FDC* (see PBS13)* £1350
1993... £1300	
— Proof *FDC* (see PBS10)* £1350	

4283

4283   Britannia. One Hundred pounds. (1 oz of fine gold, alloyed with silver) 10th
Anniversary of Britannia issue. R. The figure of Britannia standing in a chariot drawn
along the seashore by two horses, with the word 'BRITANNIA', the inscription. 'ONE
OUNCE FINE GOLD' and the date of the year. (Reverse design: Philip Nathan)

1997... £1400   1997 Proof *FDC* (Issued: 164) £1600

* Coins marked thus were originally issued in Royal Mint sets.
*** Where numbers of coins are quoted, these refer to individual coins. Additional coins were
included in sets which are listed in the appropriate section.*
NB. The spot price of gold at the time of going to press was £720 per oz.

Obverse portrait by Ian Rank-Broadley

4450   4451

4450 **Britannia. One Hundred pounds.** (1oz fine gold alloyed with silver) R. The figure of Britannia standing upon a rock in the sea, her right hand grasping a trident and her left hand resting on a shield and holding an olive branch, with the word 'BRITANNIA', the date of the year, and the inscription' ONE OUNCE FINE GOLD'. (Reverse design: Philip Nathan)

1998 Proof *FDC* (see PBS15)* ... £1350	2004 .... £1300
1999..£1300	2004 Proof *FDC* (see PBS23)* £1350
1999 Proof *FDC* (see PBS16)* ... £1350	2006 Proof *FDC* (see PBS27)* £1350
2000..£1300	2012 .... £1300
2000 Proof *FDC* (see PBS17)* ... £1350	2012 Proof *FDC* (see PBS36) £1500
2002 Proof *FDC* (see PBS19)* ... £1350	

4450A (1 oz fine gold – 0.9999) R. As 4450 above
2013

4450B (1 oz fine gold – 0.9999) R. As 4450 above but with revised inscription 'BRITANNIA
2014 1 oz 999.9 FINE GOLD'

4451 **Britannia. One Hundred pounds.** (1oz fine gold alloyed with silver) R. The figure of Britannia, as guardian, with a shield in her left hand and a trident in her right hand, accompanied by a lion and, against the background of a wave motif, the words 'ONE OUNCE FINE GOLD' to the left and 'BRITANNIA' and the date of the year to the right. (Reverse design: Philip Nathan)

2001 .... £1300   2001 Proof *FDC* (see PBS18)* £1350

4452   4453

4452 **Britannia. One Hundred pounds.** (1oz fine gold alloyed with silver) R. Helmeted head of Britannia with, to the left, the word 'BRITANNIA' and, to the right, the inscription 'ONE OUNCE FINE GOLD' and the date of the year, the whole being overlaid with a wave pattern. (Reverse design: Philip Nathan)

2003.. £1300   2003 Proof *FDC* (see PBS20)* £1350

4453 **Britannia. One Hundred pounds.** (1oz fine gold alloyed with silver) R. Seated figure of Britannia facing to the left holding a trident with a shield at her side, with the word 'BRITANNIA', the inscription 'ONE OUNCE FINE GOLD' and the date of the year. (Reverse design: Philip Nathan)

2005 Proof *FDC* (see PBS25)* £1350

* Coins marked thus were originally issued in Royal Mint sets.
NB. The spot price of gold at the time of going to press was £720 per oz.

4454   4455

4454 Britannia. One Hundred pounds. (1 oz fine gold alloyed with silver) R. Seated figure
of Britannia facing right holding a trident in her right hand and a sprig of olive in the left
hand with a lion at her feet with the inscription 'ONE OUNCE FINE GOLD' and the word
'BRITANNIA' and the date of the year (See 4505) (Reverse design: Christopher Le Brun)
2007... £1300   2007 Proof *FDC* (see PBS29)* £1350
4454A(1 oz platinum)
2007 Proof *FDC* (see 2007 set, PPBCS1)*...£1500
4455 Britannia. One Hundred pounds. (1oz fine gold alloyed with silver) R. A Standing figure
of Britannia holding a trident with a shield at her side, the folds of her dress transforming
into a wave, with the word 'BRITANNIA', and the date of the year, and the inscription
'ONE OUNCE FINE GOLD' (Reverse design: John Bergdahl)
2008.. £1300   2008 Proof *FDC* (see PBS30)* £1350
4455A(1 oz platinum)
2008 Proof *FDC* (see 2008 set, PPBCS2)* £1500

4456   4457   4458

4456 Britannia. One Hundred pounds. (1oz fine gold alloyed with silver) R. Standing figure
of Britannia in horse drawn chariot.
2009...£1300   2009 Proof *FDC* (see PBS31)* £1350
4457 Britannia. One Hundred pounds. (1oz fine gold alloyed with silver) R. A design
depicting **a** profile bust of Britannia wearing a helmet, accompanied by the name
'BRITANNIA', the inscription 'ONE OUNCE FINE GOLD' and the date '2010'.
(Reverse design: Suzie Zamit)
2010 ....£1300   2010 Proof *FDC* (Edition: 1,250 in sets)*£1350
4458 Britannia. One Hundred pounds. (1 oz fine gold alloyed with silver) R. A design
depicting a seated figure of Britannia set against a background of a rippling Union Flag
accompanied by the words 'ONE OUNCE FINE GOLD BRITANNIA, and the date
'2011'. (Reverse design: David Mach)
2011 Proof *FDC* (Edition: 3,000 including coins in sets) * £1500

* Coins marked thus were originally issued in Royal Mint sets.
NB. The spot price of gold at the time of going to press was £720 per oz.

4459

4459 Britannia. One Hundred pounds. (1 oz. of fine gold) R. Seated figure of Britannia holding a trident with a shield at her side and an owl upon her knee with the word 'BRITANNIA' and 'ONE OUNCE FINE GOLD' and the date '2013' below the figure of Britannia. (Reverse design: Robert Hunt)

2013 — Proof in gold *FDC* (0.9999) (Edition: 400 including coins in sets)*

4460 Britannia. One Hundred pounds. (1 oz of fine gold) R. A design of the standing figure of Britannia baring a trident and shield, with a lion at her feet, set against the backdrop of a globe, and with the inscription 'BRITANNIA 999.9 ONE OZ FINE GOLD 2014'. (Reverse design: Jody Clark)

2014 — Proof in gold *FDC* (0.9999) (Edition: 400 including coins in sets)*

4800

4800 Britannia. Five Hundred pounds. (5 oz of fine gold) R. Seated figure of Britannia holding a trident with a shield at her side and an owl upon her knee with the word 'BRITANNIA' and '5 oz. FINE GOLD' and the date '2013' below the figure of Britannia. (Reverse design: Robert Hunt) (Reverse design: Robert Hunt)

2013 — Proof in gold *FDC* (0.9999) (Edition: 125)..£8200

* Coins marked thus were originally issued in Royal Mint sets.
NB. The spot price of gold at the time of going to press was £720 per oz.

4801

4801 Britannia. Five Hundred pounds. (5 oz of fine gold) R A design of the standing figure
of Britannia baring a trident and shield, with a lion at her feet, set against the backdrop
of a globe, and with the inscription 'BRITANNIA 999.9 FIVE OZ FINE GOLD 2014'.
(Reverse design: Jody Clark)
2014 — Proof in gold *FDC* (0.9999) (Edition: 75)...£7500

4825 Britannia. Two thousand five hundred pounds. (1 Kilo of fine gold) R. A design of the
figure of Britannia on a textured background standing upon a rock in the sea, her right
hand grasping a trident and her left hand on a shield and holding an olive branch, with
the inscription 'BRITANNIA' (and the date of the year) 1KILO OF 999.9 FINE GOLD'
(Original reverse design: Philip Nathan)
2014 — Proof in gold *FDC*

CHINESE LUNAR YEAR SERIES – SHENGXIAO COLLECTION

4830   4831

4830 Two pounds. (1 oz 0.999 fine silver) R. A design depicting a horse prancing past the
Uffington chalk white horse, with the inscription 'YEAR OF THE HORSE. 2014' and
the Chinese symbol for horse. (Reverse design: Wuon-Gean Ho)
2014 — Proof in silver *FDC* (Edition: 8,888) £83

4830ATwo pounds. Error obverse – known as a Mule. The obverse design of The Queen used
for the £2 Silver Britannia uncirculated coin was paired with the reverse design of the
Year of the Horse £2 silver coin.
2014

4831 Two pounds. (1 oz 0.999 fine silver) R. Design depicting two Swaledale sheep, with the
inscription 'YEAR OF THE SHEEP 2015' and the Chinese symbol for sheep. (Reverse
design: Wuon-Gean Ho)
2015
— Proof in silver *FDC* (Edition: 9,888) £83
— Proof in silver with gold plating *FDC* (Edition: 4,888).........................£110

NB. The spot price of gold at the time of going to press was £720 per oz.

4840

4840 **Ten pounds.** (5 oz 0.999 fine silver) R. A design depicting a horse prancing past the Uffington chalk white horse, with the inscription 'YEAR OF THE HORSE. 2014' and the Chinese symbol for horse. (Reverse design: Wuon-Gean Ho)
2014 — Proof in silver *FDC* (Edition; 1,488) £450
Illustration shown at reduced size - actual coin diameter 65mm

4841

4841 **Ten pounds.** (5 oz 0.999 fine silver) R. Design depicting two Swaledale sheep, with the inscription 'YEAR OF THE SHEEP 2015' and the Chinese symbol for sheep. (Reverse design: Wuon-Gean Ho)
2015
— Proof in silver *FDC* (Edition: 1,088) £395
Illustration shown at reduced size - actual coin diameter 65mm

4850 **Five hundred pounds.** R. Design depicting two Swaledale sheep, with the inscription 'YEAR OF THE SHEEP 2015' and the Chinese symbol for sheep. (Reverse design: Wuon-Gean Ho)
2015
— Proof in silver *FDC* (1 Kilo)

4860   4861

4860 Ten pounds. (1/10 oz 0.9999 fine gold) R. A design depicting a horse prancing past the Uffington chalk white horse, with the inscription 'YEAR OF THE HORSE. 2014' and the Chinese symbol for horse. (Reverse design: Wuon-Gean Ho)
2014 — BU (Edition; 2,888) £225

4861 Ten pounds. (1/10 oz 0.9999 fine gold) R. Design depicting two Swaledale sheep, with the inscription 'YEAR OF THE SHEEP 2015' and the Chinese symbol for sheep. (Reverse design: Wuon-Gean Ho)
2015 — BU (Edition: 2,888) £225

4870

4870 One hundred pounds. (1 oz 0.9999 fine gold) R. A design depicting a horse prancing past the Uffington chalk white horse, with the inscription 'YEAR OF THE HORSE . 2014' and the Chinese symbol for horse. (Reverse design: Wuon-Gean Ho)
2014
— Gold bullion type (Edition: 30,000)
— Proof in gold *FDC* (Edition; 888) £1950

4871

4871 One hundred pounds. (1 oz 0.999 fine gold) R. Design depicting two Swaledale sheep, with the inscription 'YEAR OF THE SHEEP 2015' and the Chinese symbol for sheep. (Reverse design: Wuon-Gean Ho)
2015
— Proof in gold *FDC* (Edition: 888) £1950

NB. The spot price of gold at the time of going to press was £720 per oz.

4881 Five hundred pounds. (5 oz. 0.9999 fine gold) R. A design depicting a horse prancing past the Uffington chalk white horse, with the inscription 'YEAR OF THE HORSE . 2014' and the Chinese symbol for horse. (Reverse design: Wuon-Gean Ho)
2014 — Proof in gold *FDC* (Edition:) £7500

4882

4882 Five hundred pounds. R. Design depicting two Swaledale sheep, with the inscription 'YEAR OF THE SHEEP 2015' and the Chinese symbol for sheep. (Reverse design: Wuon-Gean Ho)
2015
— Proof in gold *FDC* (5 oz. fine gold) (Edition: 38) £7500
Illustration shown at reduced size - actual coin diameter 65mm

4885 One thousand pounds. (1 Kilo 0.9999 fine gold) R. Design depicting two Swaledale sheep, with the inscription 'YEAR OF THE SHEEP 2015' and the Chinese symbol for sheep. (Reverse design: Wuon-Gean Ho)
2015
— Proof in gold *FDC* (Edition:)

WORLD WAR ONE – A SERIES OF DESIGNS MARKING THE OUTBREAK OF WAR TO THE ARMISTICE

4764

4764 Five pound. (crown). R. A design depicting British troops waving to crowds as they embark on a ship with the inscription '1914 THE FIRST WORLD WAR 1918. BEF' with the edge inscription 'SALUTE THE OLD CONTEMPTIBLES'. (Reverse design: John Bergdahl)
2014 — Proof in silver *FDC* (Edition: 1,914 in sets, see PSS60)
— Proof in gold *FDC*

NB. The spot price of gold at the time of going to press was £720 per oz.

4765   4766

4765 **Five pound.** (crown). R. A design depicting three Howitzers with the inscription '1914 THE FIRST WORLD WAR 1918' and the edge inscription 'NEW AND FURIOUS BOMBARDMENT' (Reverse design: Edwina Ellis)

     2014 — Proof in silver *FDC* (Edition: 1,914 in sets, see PSS60)

     —   Proof in gold *FDC*

4766 **Five pound.** (crown). R. A design depicting an effigy of Walter Tull in uniform with soldiers walking out over no man's land and the inscription '1914 THE FIRST WORLD WAR 1918' and 'WALTER TULL' around the coin, separated by poppy flowers with barbed wire with the edge inscription' A HERO ON AND OFF THE FIELD'. (Reverse design: David Cornell)

     2014 — Proof in silver *FDC* (Edition: 1,914 in sets, see PSS60)

     —   Proof in gold *FDC*

4767

4767 **Five pound.** (crown). R. A design depicting a naval gun being loaded on board the deck of a battleship with the inscription '1914 THE FIRST WORLD WAR 1918. NAVY' and the edge inscription 'THE KING'S SHIPS WERE AT SEA'.(Reverse design: David Rowlands)

     2014 — Proof in silver *FDC* (Edition: 1,914 in sets, see PSS60)

     —   Proof in gold *FDC*

NB. The spot price of gold at the time of going to press was £720 per oz.

4768

4768 Five pound. (crown). R. A design depicting a man putting up propaganda posters onto a
  brick wall with the inscription '1914 THE FIRST WORLD WAR 1918' and the edge
  inscription 'FOLLOW ME! YOUR COUNTRY NEEDS YOU'
  2014 — Proof in silver *FDC* (Edition: 1,914 in sets, see PSS60)
  —   Proof in gold FDC

4769

4769 Five pound. (crown). R. A design depicting a woman working fields with a plough with
  the inscription '1914 THE FIRST WORLD WAR 1918. HOMEFRONT' and the edge
  inscription 'SPEED THE PLOUGH AND THE WOMAN WHO DRIVES IT'. (Reverse
  design: David Rowlands)
  2014 – Proof in silver FDC (Edition: 1,914 in sets, see PSS60)
  —   Proof in gold FDC

NB. The spot price of gold at the time of going to press was £720 per oz.

The Royal Mint plan to issue a considerable number of coins to mark the London 2012 Olympic and Paralympic Games. It has been decided that it will be easier for collectors if these coins are grouped together rather than be included with other coins of the same denomination. As a consequence the £2 coins issued in 2008 (previously listed as 4585 and 4586) have been renumbered and are now part of the Olympic group.

LONDON 2012 OLYMPIC AND PARALYMPIC GAMES

As part of their Programme of Olympic commemorative issues the Royal Mint has struck and released into circulation a series of 29 different 50 pence coins and details are given below. In addition to the circulating coins there is a series of numbered coin packs each containing the cupro-nickel versions of the coins but of higher quality. There are also sterling silver brilliant uncirculating examples.

The artist for each coin in the series has received a gold version of their design and a further example has been placed in the Mint museum. No value is shown at the present time.

4960   4961

4960 Fifty pence. To commemorate the London 2012 Olympic and Paralympic Games. R. A design which depicts an athlete clearing a high jump bar, with the London 2012 logo above and the denomination '50 pence' below. (Reverse design: Florence Jackson) 2009

  — Specimen in presentation folder (Edition: 100,000) £3
  — Gold FDC – presented to the artist
  2011 ....£1
  — Specimen in card (3/29) £3
  — Specimen in presentation folder signed by Daley Thompson (Edition: 500) £50
  — Specimen in presentation folder signed by Dame Kelly Holmes (Edition: 500) £50
  — Specimen in presentation folder signed by Lord Sebastian Coe (Edition: 500) £50
  — Silver BU (Edition: 30,000) £35

4961 Fifty pence. To commemorate the London 2012 Olympic and Paralympic Games. R. A design which depicts a cyclist in a velodrome, with the London Olympic logo above and the denomination '50 PENCE' below. (Reverse design: Theo Crutchley- Mack) 2010

  — Gold FDC – presented to the artist
  2011 ....£1
  Specimen in card (9/29) £3
  — Silver BU (Edition: 30,000) £35

4962   4963

4962 **Fifty pence.** To commemorate the London 2012 Olympic and Paralympic Games. ℞.
A design which depicts a swimmer submerged in water, with the London Olympic logo
above and the denomination '50 PENCE' below. (Reverse design: Jonathan Olliffe)
2011 .... £1   Specimen in card (1/29) £3
— Silver BU (Edition: 30,000) ..... £35   — Gold *FDC* – presented to the artist

4963 **Fifty pence.** To commemorate the London 2012 Olympic and Paralympic Games. ℞. A
design which depicts a bow being drawn, with the London Olympic logo above and the
denomination '50 PENCE' below. (Reverse design: Piotr Powaga)
2011 .... £1   Specimen in card (2/29) £3
— Silver BU (Edition: 30,000) ..... £35   — Gold *FDC* – presented to the artist

4964   4965

4964 **Fifty pence.** To commemorate the London 2012 Olympic and Paralympic Games. ℞. A
design which depicts a shuttlecock and a diagram of badminton actions, with the London
Olympic logo above and the denomination '50 PENCE' below. (Reverse design: Emma
Kelly)
2011 .... £1   Specimen in card (4/29) £3
— Silver BU (Edition: 30,000) ..... £35   — Gold *FDC* – presented to the artist

4965 **Fifty pence.** To commemorate the London 2012 Olympic and Paralympic Games. ℞. A
design which depicts basketball players against a textured background of a large basketball,
with the London Olympic logo above and the denomination '50 PENCE' below. (Reverse
design: Sarah Payne)
2011 .... £1   Specimen in card (5/29) £3
— Silver BU (Edition: 30,000) ..... £35   — Gold *FDC* – presented to the artist

4966   4967

4966 Fifty pence. To commemorate the London 2012 Olympic and Paralympic Games. R. A design
which depicts a boccia player in a wheelchair throwing a ball, with the London Olympic logo
above and the denomination "50 PENCE" below. (Reverse design: Justin Chung)
2011 .... £1   Specimen in card (6/29) £3
— Silver BU (Edition: 30,000) ..... £35   — Gold *FDC* – presented to the artist

4967 Fifty pence. To commemorate the London 2012 Olympic and Paralympic Games. R. A design
which depicts a pair of boxing gloves against the background of a boxing ring, with the London
Olympic logo above and the denomination "50 PENCE" below. (Reverse design: Shane Abery)
2011 .... £1   Specimen in card (7/29) £3
— Silver BU (Edition: 30,000) ..... £35   — Gold *FDC* – presented to the artist

4968   4969

4968 Fifty pence. To commemorate the London 2012 Olympic and Paralympic Games. R. A
design which depicts a figure in a canoe on a slalom course, with the London Olympic logo
above and the denomination "50 PENCE" below. (Reverse design: Timothy Lees)
2011 .... £1   Specimen in card (8/29) £3
— Silver BU (Edition: 30,000) ..... £35   — Gold *FDC* – presented to the artist

4969 Fifty pence. To commemorate the London 2012 Olympic and Paralympic Games. R. A
design which depicts a horse and rider jumping over a fence, with the London Olympic logo
above and the denomination "50 PENCE" below. (Reverse design: Thomas Babbage)
2011 .... £1   Specimen in card (10/29) £3
— Silver BU (Edition: 30,000) ..... £35   — Gold *FDC* – presented to the artist

4970

4971

4970 Fifty pence. To commemorate the London 2012 Olympic and Paralympic Games. R. A design which depicts two figures fencing, with the London Olympic logo above and the denomination "50 PENCE" below. (Reverse design: Ruth Summerfield)

2011 .... £1   Specimen in card (11/29) £3
— Silver BU (Edition: 30,000) ..... £35   — Gold *FDC* – presented to the artist

4971 Fifty pence. To commemorate the London 2012 Olympic and Paralympic Games. R. A diagrammatic explanation of the offside rule in football, with the London Olympic logo above and the denomination "50 PENCE" below. (Reverse design: Neil Wolfson)

2011 .... £1   Specimen in card (12/29) £3
— Silver BU (Edition: 30,000) ..... £35   — Gold *FDC* – presented to the artist

4972

4973

4972 Fifty pence. To commemorate the London 2012 Olympic and Paralympic Games. R. A design which depicts a goalball player throwing a ball, with the London Olympic logo above and the denomination "50 PENCE" below. (Reverse design: Jonathan Wren)

2011 .... £1   Specimen in card (13/29) £3
— Silver BU (Edition: 30,000) ..... £35   — Gold *FDC* – presented to the artist

4973 Fifty pence. To commemorate the London 2012 Olympic and Paralympic Games. R. A design which depicts a gymnast with a ribbon, with the London Olympic logo above and the denomination "50 PENCE" below. (Reverse design: Jonathan Olliffe)

2011 .... £1   Specimen in card (14/29) £3
— Silver BU (Edition: 30,000) ..... £35   — Gold *FDC* – presented to the artist

4974   4975

4974 **Fifty pence.** To commemorate the London 2012 Olympic and Paralympic Games. ℞. A design which depicts a handball player throwing a ball against a background of a handball court, with the London Olympic logo above and the denomination '50 PENCE' below. (Reverse design: Natasha Ratcliffe)

2011 .... £1   Specimen in card (15/29) £3
—   Silver BU (Edition: 30,000) ..... £35   —   Gold *FDC* – presented to the artist

4975 **Fifty pence.** To commemorate the London 2012 Olympic and Paralympic Games. ℞. A design which depicts two hockey players challenging for the ball, with the London Olympic logo above and the denomination "50 PENCE" below. (Reverse design: Robert Evans)

2011 .... £1   Specimen in card (16/29) £3
—   Silver BU (Edition: 30,000) ..... £35   —   Gold *FDC* – presented to the artist

4976   4977

4976 **Fifty pence.** To commemorave the London 2012 Olympic and Paralympic Games. ℞. A depiction of a judo throw, with the London Olympic logo above and the denomination '50 PENCE' below. (Reverse design: David Cornell)

2011 .... £1   Specimen in card (17/29) £3
—   Silver BU (Edition: 30,000) ..... £35   —   Gold *FDC* – presented to the artist

4977 **Fifty pence.** To commemorate the London 2012 Olympic and Paralympic Games. ℞. A montage of the five sports which form the modern pentathlon, with the London Olympic logo above and the denomination '50 PENCE' below. (Reverse design: Daniel Brittain)

2011 .... £1   Specimen in card (18/29) £3
—   Silver BU (Edition: 30,000) ..... £35   —   Gold *FDC* – presented to the artist

4978   4979

4978 **Fifty pence.** To commemorate the London 2012 Olympic and Paralympic Games. R. A design which depicts a rowing boat accompanied by a number of words associated with the Olympic movement, with the London Olympic logo above and the denomination '50 PENCE' below. (Reverse design: David Podmore)

2011 ....£1
— Specimen in card (19/29)...£3
— Specimen in presentation folder signed by Sir Steve Redgrave (Edition: 500)............£50
— Silver BU (Edition: 30,000)..£35

4979 **Fifty pence.** To commemorate the London 2012 Olympic and Paralympic Games. R. A design which depicts three sailing boats accompanied by a map of the coast of Weymouth, with the London Olympic logo above and the denomination '50 PENCE' below. (Reverse design: Bruce Rushin)

2011 .... £1   Specimen in card (20/29)............................£3
— Silver BU (Edition: 30,000)..... £35   — Gold *FDC* – presented to the artist

4980   4981

4980 **Fifty pence.** To commemorate the London 2012 Olympic and Paralympic Games. R. A design which depicts a figure shooting, with the London Olympic logo above and the denomination '50 PENCE' below. (Reverse design: Pravin Dewdhory)

2011 .... £1   Specimen in card (21/29)............................£3
— Silver BU (Edition: 30,000)..... £35   — Gold *FDC* – presented to the artist

4981 **Fifty pence.** To commemorate the London 2012 Olympic and Paralympic Games. R. A design which depicts two table tennis bats against the background of a table and net, with the London Olympic logo above and the denomination "50 PENCE" below. (Reverse design: Alan Linsdell)

2011 .... £1   Specimen in card (22/29)............................£3
— Silver BU (Edition: 30,000)..... £35   — Gold *FDC* – presented to the artist

4982   4983

4982 Fifty pence. To commemorate the London 2012 Olympic and Paralympic Games. R. A design which depicts two athletes engaged in Taekwondo, with the London Olympic logo above and the denomination "50 PENCE" below. (Reverse design: David Gibbons)

2011 .... £1   Specimen in card (23/29) £3
—   Silver BU (Edition: 30,000) ..... £35   —   Gold *FDC* – presented to the artist

4983 Fifty pence. To commemorate the London 2012 Olympic and Paralympic Games. R. A design which depicts a tennis net and tennis ball, with the London Olympic logo above and the denomination "50 PENCE" below. (Reverse design: Tracy Baines)

2011 .... £1   Specimen in card (24/29) £3
—   Silver BU (Edition: 30,000) ..... £35   —   Gold *FDC* – presented to the artist

4984   4985

4984 Fifty pence. To commemorate the London 2012 Olympic and Paralympic Games. R. A montage of the three sports which form the triathlon, with the London Olympic logo above and the denomination "50 PENCE" below. (Reverse design: Sarah Harvey)

2011 .... £1   Specimen in card (25/29) £3
—   Silver BU (Edition: 30,000) ..... £35   —   Gold *FDC* – presented to the artist

4985 Fifty pence. To commemorate the London 2012 Olympic and Paralympic Games. R. A design which depicts three figures playing beach volleyball, with the London Olympic logo above and the denomination "50 PENCE" below. (Reverse design: Daniela Boothman)

2011 .... £1   Specimen in card (26/29) £3
—   Silver BU (Edition: 30,000) ..... £35   —   Gold *FDC* – presented to the artist

4986   4987

4986 Fifty pence. To commemorate the London 2012 Olympic and Paralympic Games. R.
A design which depicts the outline of a weightlifter starting a lift, with the London
Olympic logo above and the denomination "50 PENCE" below. (Reverse design:
Rob Shakespeare)
2011 ....£1   Specimen in card (27/29) ....
£3
— Silver BU (Edition: 30,000)...£35   — Gold *FDC* – presented to the artist

4987 Fifty pence. To commemorate the London 2012 Olympic and Paralympic Games. R. A
design which depicts a wheelchair rugby player in action, with the London Olympic logo
above and the denomination "50 PENCE" below. (Reverse design: Natasha Ratcliffe)
2011 ....£1   Specimen in card (28/29) ....
£3
— Silver BU (Edition: 30,000)...£35   — Gold *FDC* – presented to the artist

4988

4988 Fifty pence. To commemorate the London 2012 Olympic and Paralympic Games. R. A
design which depicts two figures wrestling in a stadium, with the London Olympic logo
above and the denomination "50 PENCE" below. (Reverse design: Roderick Enriquez)
2011 ....£1   Specimen in card (29/29) ....
£3
— Silver BU (Edition: 30,000)...£35   — Gold *FDC* – presented to the artist

4951   4952

4951 Two pounds. (Previously listed as 4585) Centenary of the Olympic Games of 1908 held
in London. R. A running track on which is superimposed the date '1908' accompanied
by the denomination 'TWO POUNDS' and the date '2008', the whole design being
encircled by the inscription 'LONDON OLYMPIC CENTENARY' with the edge
inscription 'THE 4TH OLYMPIAD LONDON' (Reverse design: Thomas T Docherty)
2008 .... £5
—   Specimen in presentation folder (Issued: 29,594) £10
—   Proof *FDC* (in 2008 set, see PS93)* £15
—   Proof in Silver *FDC* (Issued: 8,023) £35
—   Proof piedfort in silver *FDC* (Edition: 5,000).................................£55
—   Proof in gold *FDC* (Issued: 1,908 including coins in sets) £700

4952 Two pounds. (Previously listed as 4586) London Olympic Handover Ceremony. R.
The Olympic flag being passed from one hand to another, encircled by the inscription
'BEIJING 2008 LONDON 2012' and with the London 2012 logo below with the edge
inscription 'I CALL UPON THE YOUTH OF THE WORLD' (Reverse design: Royal
Mint Engraving Team)
2008 ....£5
—   Specimen in presentation folder (Edition: 250,000) £10
—   Proof in Silver *FDC* (Issued: 30,000) £38
—   Proof piedfort in silver *FDC* (Issued: 3,000) £60
—   Proof in gold *FDC* (Edition: 3,250 including coins in sets)...............£700

4953

4953 Two pounds. London to Rio Olympic Handover coin. R. A design which depicts a
baton being passed from one hand to another, accompanied by the conjoined Union
and Brazilian Flags. The reverse design is set against the background of a running track
motif, with the London 2012 logo above and the surrounding inscription 'LONDON
2012 RIO 2016'. With the edge inscription 'I CALL UPON THE YOUTH OF THE
WORLD'. (Reverse design: Jonathan Olliffe)
2012
—   Specimen in presentation card...£10
—   Proof in silver *FDC* (Edition: 12,000) £60
—   Proof piedfort in silver *FDC* (Edition: 2,000).................................£105
—   Proof in gold *FDC* (Edition: 1,200) £1195

4920

4920 Five pounds. (crown) UK countdown to 2012 Olympic Games. R. In the centre a
depiction of two swimmers as faceted figures accompanied by the number '3' with
a section of a clock face to the right and the London 2012 logo to the left printed in
coloured ink on the precious metal versions and surrounded by a plan view of the main
Olympic Stadium incorporating the date '2009' with the words 'COUNTDOWN' above
and the inscription 'XXX OLYMPIAD' below. (Reverse design: Claire Aldridge) (Obv.
as 4556)

2009 (Edition: 500,000) £8
— Specimen in presentation folder (Edition: 500,000) £10
— Proof in silver *FDC* (Issued: 30,000) £95
— Proof piedfort in silver *FDC* (Issued: 6,000) £175
— Proof in gold *FDC* (Edition: 4,000) £2000

4921

4921 Five pounds. (crown) UK countdown to 2012 Olympic Games. R. In the centre a
depiction of two runners as faceted figures accompanied by the number '2' with a section
of a clock face to the right and the London 2012 logo to the left printed in coloured
ink on the precious meta versions and surrounded by a plan view of the main Olympic
Stadium incorporating the date '2010' with the words 'COUNTDOWN' above and the
inscription 'XXX OLYMPIAD' below.(Reverse design: Claire Aldridge) (Obv. as 4556)

2010
— Specimen in presentation card (Edition: 250,000) £8
— Specimen in presentation folder (Edition: 250,000) £10
— Proof in silver *FDC* (Edition: 30,000) £80
— Proof piedfort in silver *FDC* (Edition: 4,000) £200
— Proof in gold *FDC* (Edition: 3,000) £2000

4922

4922 Five pounds. (crown) UK countdown to 2012 Olympic Games. R. In the centre a
depiction of a cyclist as a faceted figure, accompanied by the number '1' with a section
of a clock face to the right, below and to the left, and the London 2012 logo to the right
printed in coloured ink on the precious metal versions and surrounded by a plan view of
the main Olympic Stadium incorporating the date '2011' with the words
'COUNTDOWN' above and the inscription 'XXX OLYMPIAD' below. (Reverse design:
Claire Aldridge)
2011
— Specimen in presentation card   (Edition: 250,000) £8
— Specimen in presentation folder (Edition: 250,000)..£10
— Proof in silver *FDC* (Edition: 30,000) £100
— Proof piedfort in silver *FDC* (Edition: 4,000) £175
— Proof in gold *FDC* (Edition: 3,000)..£2880

4923

4923 Five pounds. (crown) UK countdown to 2012 Olympic Games. R. A depiction of three
athletes as faceted figures standing on a victory podium, with a section of a clock-face to
the right, to the left and above, and the London 2012 logo to the right. The reverse design
is surrounded by a plan view of the main Olympic Stadium, incorporating the date '2012'
at the top, and the word 'COUNTDOWN' above and the inscription 'XXX OLYMPIAD'
below. (Reverse design: Claire Aldridge)
2012
— Specimen in presentation card   (Edition: 250,000) £8
— Specimen in presentation folder (Edition: 250,000) £13
— Proof in silver *FDC* (Edition: 30,000) £100
— Proof piedfort in silver *FDC* (Edition: 4,000)..£175
— Proof in gold *FDC* (Edition: 3,000) £2880

4924

4924 Five pounds. (crown) The London 2012 Olympic Games. ℞. An image of the skyline of
some of the most well-known landmarks and buildings in London reflected in the River
Thames, with the inscription 'LONDON 2012' above. Surrounding the skyline image is
a selection of sports from the London 2012 Games with the London 2012 logo at the top.
(Reverse design: Saiman Miah)
2012
—   Specimen in presentation folder £15
—   Proof in silver *FDC* (Edition: 100,000) £100
—   Proof in silver with gold plating *FDC* (Edition: 12,500) £125
—   Proof piedfort in silver *FDC* (Edition: 7,000)..£175
—   Proof in gold *FDC* (Edition: 5,000) £2880

4925

4925 Five pounds. (crown) The London 2012 Paralympic Games. ℞. A design showing
segments of a target, a spoked wheel, a stopwatch and the clock face of the Palace of
Westminster. The inscription 'LONDON 2012' appears on the target and the London
2012 Paralympic logo appears on the stopwatch. On the gold and silver coins the London
Paralympic logo will be printed in coloured ink , while on the cupro-nickel coin the logo
will be struck into the surface. (Reverse design: Pippa Anderson)
2012
—   Specimen in presentation folder (Edition: 250,000) £15
—   Proof in silver *FDC* (Edition: 10,000) £100
—   Proof in silver with gold plating *FDC* (Edition: 3,000) £125
—   Proof piedfort in silver *FDC* (Edition: 2,012)..£175
—   Proof in gold *FDC* (Edition: 2,012) £2880

4930

4930 Five pounds. (crown) The Mind of Britain. R. A depiction of the clock-face of the Palace of Westminster accompanied by the London 2012 logo, printed in coloured ink and a quotation From Walter Bagehot, 'NATIONS TOUCH AT THEIR SUMMITS'. (Reverse design: Shane Greeves and the Royal Mint Engraving Department)
2009
—   Proof *FDC* (Edition: 100,000)£20   —   Proof silver *FDC* (Edition: 95,000) £100

4931

4931 Five pounds. (crown). The Mind of Britain. R. A depiction of Stonehenge accompanied by the London 2012 logo, printed in coloured ink on the silver version and a quotation from William Blake 'GREAT THINGS ARE DONE WHEN MEN AND MOUNTAINS MEET' (Reverse design: Shane Greeves and the Royal Mint Engraving Department)
2009
—   Proof silver *FDC* (Edition: 95,000) £100

4932   4933

4932 **Five pounds.** (crown). The Mind of Britain. R. A depiction of the Angel of the North accompanied   by the London 2012 logo printed in coloured ink on the silver version and a quotation from William Shakespeare 'I HAVE TOUCHED THE HIGHEST POINT OF MY GREATNESS' (Reverse design: Shane Greeves and the Royal Mint Engraving Department) 2009

— Proof silver *FDC* (Edition: 95,000) £100

4933 **Five pounds.** (crown). The Mind of Britain. R. A depiction of the Flying Scotsman accompanied   by the London 2012 logo printed in coloured ink on the silver version and a quotation from William Shakespeare 'TRUE HOPE IS SWIFT' (Reverse design: Shane Greeves and the Royal Mint Engraving Department) 2009

— Proof silver *FDC* (Edition: 95,000) £100

4934

4934 **Five pounds.** (crown). The Mind of Britain. R. A depiction of Eduardo Paolozzi's sculpture of Isaac Newton North accompanied by the London 2012 logo printed in coloured ink on the silver version and a quotation from William Shakespeare 'MAKE NOT YOUR THOUGHTS YOUR PRISONS' (Reverse design: Shane Greeves and the Royal Mint Engraving Department) 2009

— Proof silver *FDC* (Edition: 95,000) £100

4935

4935 **Five pounds.** (crown). The Mind of Britain. R. A depiction of the Globe Theatre
accompanied by the London 2012 logo printed in coloured ink on the silver version and a
quotation from William Shakespeare 'WE ARE SUCH STUFF AS DREAMS ARE MADE
ON' (Reverse design: Shane Greeves and the Royal Mint Engraving Department)
2009
— Proof silver *FDC* (Edition: 95,000) £100

4936   4937

4936 **Five pounds.** (crown). The Body of Britain. R. A depiction of Rhossili Bay accompanied
by the London 2012 logo printed in coloured ink, and a quotation from William Blake
'TO SEE A WORLD IN A GRAIN OF SAND' (Reverse design: Shane Greeves and the
Royal Mint Engraving Department)
2010
— Proof silver *FDC* (Edition: 95,000) £100
4937 **Five pounds.** (crown). The Body of Britain. R. A depiction of Giant's Causeway
accompanied by the London 2012 logo printed in coloured ink, and a quotation from
Alice Oswald 'WHEN THE STONE BEGAN TO DREAM' (Reverse design: Shane
Greeves and the Royal Mint Engraving Department)
2010
— Proof silver *FDC* (Edition: 95,000) £100

4938   4939

4938 **Five pounds.** (crown). The Body of Britain R. A depiction of the River Thames accompanied
by the London 2012 logo printed in coloured ink, and a quotation from Percy Bysshe Shelley,
'TAMELESS, AND SWIFT AND PROUD' (Reverse design: Shane Greeves and the Royal
Mint Engraving Department)
2010
—   Proof silver *FDC* (Edition: 95,000).. £100

4939 **Five pounds.** (crown). The Body of Britain. R. A depiction of a barn owl accompanied by
the London 2012 logo printed in coloured ink, and a quotation from Samuel Johnson 'THE
NATURAL FLIGHTS OF THE HUMAN MIND' (Reverse design: Shane Greeves and the
Royal Mint Engraving Department)
2010
—   Proof silver *FDC* (Edition: 95,000)... £100

4940   4941

4940 **Five pounds.** (crown). The Body of Britain. R. A depiction of oak leaves and an acorn
accompanied by the London 2012 logo printed in coloured ink, and a quotation from Alfred,
Lord Tennyson, 'TO STRIVE, TO SEEK......AND NOT TO YIELD' (Reverse design: Shane
Greeves and the Royal Mint Engraving Department)
2010
—   Proof silver *FDC* (Edition: 95,000)... £100

4941 **Five pounds.** (crown). The Body of Britain. R. A depiction of a weather-vane accompanied by
the London 2012 logo printed in coloured ink, and a quotation from Charlotte Bronte, NEVER
MAY A CLOUD COME O'ER THE SUNSHINE OF YOUR MIND' (Reverse design:
Shane Greeves and the Royal Mint Engraving Department)
2010
—   Proof silver *FDC* (Edition: 95,000)... £100

4942   4943

4942   **Five pounds.** (crown). The Spirit of Britain. R. A depiction of the intertwined national emblems of England, Scotland, Wales and Northern Ireland accompanied by the London 2012 logo, printed in coloured ink, and a quotation from John Lennon, 'AND THE WORLD WILL BE ONE' (Reverse design: Shane Greeves and the Royal Mint Engraving Department) 2010

    —   Proof silver *FDC* (Edition: 95,000).. £100

4943   **Five pounds.** (crown). The Spirit of Britain. R. A depiction of the White Rabbit from Lewis Carroll's *Alice in Wonderland* accompanied by the London 2012 logo, printed in coloured ink, and a quotation from T S Eliot, 'ALL TOUCHED BY A COMMON GENIUS' (Reverse design: Shane Greeves and the Royal Mint Engraving Department) 2010

    —   Proof silver *FDC* (Edition: 95,000).. £100

4944   4945

4944   **Five pounds.** (crown). The Spirit of Britain. R. A view down the Mall of cheering crowds accompanied by the London 2012 logo, printed in coloured ink, and a quotation from Alfred, Lord Tennyson, 'KIND HEARTS ARE MORE THAN CORONETS' (Reverse design: Shane Greeves and the Royal Mint Engraving Department) 2010

    —   Proof *FDC* (Edition; 100,000)...£20

    —   Proof silver *FDC* (Edition: 95,000)...£100

4945   **Five pounds.** (crown). The Spirit of Britain. R. A DEPICTION OF THE STATUE OF Winston Churchill in Parliament Square accompanied by the London 2012 logo, printed in coloured ink, and a quotation from Anita Roddick, 'BE DARING, BE FIRST, BE DIFFERENT, BE JUST' (Reverse design: Shane Greeves and the Royal Mint Engraving Department) 2010

    —   Proof *FDC* (Edition; 100,000)...£20

    —   Proof silver *FDC* (Edition: 95,000)...£100

4946

4946 Five pounds. (crown).The Spirit of Britain. ℞ An arrangement of musical instruments based on a well known sculpture accompanied by the London 2012 logo, printed in coloured ink, and a quotation from John Lennon and Paul McCartney, 'ALL YOU NEED IS LOVE'. (Reverse design: Shane Greeves and the Royal Mint Engraving Department) 2010

—   Proof silver *FDC* (Edition: 95,000) £100

4947

4947 Five pounds. (crown).The Spirit of Britain. ℞. An image of the nineteenth-century anti-slavery campaigner Equiano accompanied by the London 2012 logo, printed in coloured ink, and a quotation from William Shakespeare, 'TO THINE OWN SELF BE TRUE'. (Reverse design: Shane Greeves and the Royal Mint Engraving Department) 2010

—   Proof silver *FDC* (Edition: 95,000) £100

4950

4950 Ten pounds. (Five ounce). R. A design of the winged horse Pegasus rearing on its hind
legs surrounded by the inscription 'LONDON OLYMPIC GAMES', and the London 2012
logo and the date '2012'.(Reverse design: Christopher Le Brun)
2012
— Proof in 0.999 fine silver *FDC* (Edition: 7,500) £525
— Proof in 0.999 fine gold *FDC* (Edition: 500) £11500
Illustration shown at reduced size – actual coin diameter 65 mm.

4905

4905 Twenty five pounds. Faster. R. An image of Diana accompanied by a depiction of the
sport of cycling, specifically pursuit racing ,with Olympic Rings above, the name 'DIANA'
to the left, the Latin word for faster 'CITIUS', to the right, and the inscription 'LONDON
2012' below. (Reverse design: John Bergdahl)
2010
— Proof in gold *FDC* (Edition: 20,000) £600

4906

4906 Twenty five pounds. Faster. R. An image of Mercury accompanied by a depiction of
the sport of running, with Olympic Rings above, the name 'MERCURY' to the left, the
Latin word for faster 'CITIUS', to the right, and the inscription 'LONDON 2012' below.
(Reverse design: John Bergdahl)
2010
— Proof in gold *FDC* (Edition: 20,000) £600

4907

4907 Twenty five pounds. Higher. R. An image of Apollo accompanied by a depiction of the sport of rhythmic gymnastics, with Olympic Rings above, the name 'APOLLO' to the left, the Latin word for higher 'ALTIUS', to the right, and the inscription 'LONDON 2012' below. (Reverse design: John Bergdahl)

2011
— Proof in gold *FDC* (Edition: 20,000 including coins in sets) £600

4908   4909   4910

4908 Twenty five pounds. Higher. R. An image of Juno accompanied by a depiction of the sport of pole vaulting, with Olympic Rings above, the name 'JUNO' to the left, the Latin word for higher 'ALTIUS', to the right, and the inscription 'LONDON 2012' below. (Reverse design: John Bergdahl)

2011
— Proof in gold *FDC* (Edition: 20,000 including coins in sets) £600

4909 Twenty five pounds. Stronger. R. An image of Vulcan accompanied by a depiction of the sport of hammer throwing, with the Olympic Rings above, the name 'VULCAN' to the left, and the Latin word for stronger 'FORTIUS', to the right, and the inscription 'LONDON 2012' below. (Reverse design: John Bergdahl)

2012
— Proof in gold *FDC* (Edition: 20,000 including coins in sets) £600

4910 Twenty five pounds. Stronger. R. An image of Minerva accompanied by a depiction Of the sport of javelin throwing, with the Olympic Rings above, the name 'MINERVA' to the left , the Latin word for stronger, 'FORTIUS', to the right, and the inscription 'LONDON 2012@ below. (Reverse design: John Bergdahl)

2012
— Proof in gold *FDC* (Edition: 20,000 including coins in sets) £600

4915

4915 One hundred pounds. Faster. R. An image of Neptune, accompanied by a depiction of the sport of sailing, with the Olympic Rings above, the name 'NEPTUNE' to the left, the Latin word for faster 'CITIUS' to the right, and the inscription 'LONDON 2012' below. (Reverse design: John Bergdahl)
2010
—   Proof in gold *FDC* (Edition: 7,500 including coins in sets)...............................£2300

4916

4916 One hundred pounds. Higher. R. An image of Jupiter, accompanied by a depiction of the sport of diving, with the Olympic Rings above, the name 'JUPITER' to the left, the Latin word for higher 'ALTIUS' to the right, and the inscription 'LONDON 2012' below. (Reverse design: John Bergdahl)
2011
—   Proof in gold *FDC** (Edition: 7,500 including coins in sets)...........................£2300

4917

4917 One hundred pounds. Stronger. R. An image of Mars accompanied by a depiction of the sport of boxing, with the Olympic Rings above, the name 'MARS' to the left, the Latin word for stronger, 'FORTIUS', to the right, and the inscription 'LONDON 2012' below. (Reverse design: John Bergdahl)
2012
—   Proof in gold *FDC* (Edition: 7,500 including coins in sets).......................£2300

4920

4918 Five hundred pounds. (One kilo). R. A design consisting of celebratory pennants and the inscription 'XXX OLYMPIAD' surrounded by the epigram 'UNITE OUR DREAMS TO MAKE THE WORLD A TEAM OF TEAMS' (Reverse design: Tom Phillips) 2012
— Proof in silver (Edition: 2,012) £3000
Illustration shown at reduced size – actual coin diameter 100 mm

4921

4919 One thousand pounds. (One kilo). R. A design depicting individual pieces of sporting equipment encircled by a laurel of victory. (Reverse design: Sir Anthony Caro) 2012
— Proof in gold (Edition: 60) £100000
Illustration shown at reduced size – actual coin diameter 100 mm

The practice of issuing annual sets of coins was started by the Royal Mint in 1970 when a set of the £SD coins was issued as a souvenir prior to Decimalisation. There are now regular issues of brilliant uncirculated coin sets as well as proofs in base metal, and issues in gold and silver. In order to simplify the numbering system, and to allow for the continuation of the various issues in the future, the Prefix letters have been changed. The base metal proof sets will continue the series of numbers from the 1970 set, PS20. Other sets, such as those of uncirculated coins, silver and gold now have their numbering series commencing with number 01 in each case.

In addition to the annual sets of uncirculated and proofs coins sold by the Royal Mint to collectors and dealers, the Mint has produced specially packaged sets and single coins for companies. No details are made available of these issues and therefore no attempt has been made to include them in the listings below. The Mint also sells 'Christening' and 'Wedding' sets in distinctive packaging but the numbers circulating in the market are relatively modest and of limited appeal after the year of issue.

The Mint has recently offered sets of coins to collectors that consist of coins obtained from the market e.g. silver proofs, crowns and gold sovereigns showing different portraits. Although these are available in limited numbers from the Mint, it has been decided not to list them in the section devoted to sets.

Following the comprehensive review of the layout, it has been decided to move the folder containing the two 50 pence coins of 1992 to the list below of uncirculated coins. This was formerly included as 4352A, and is now US13 with all subsequent numbers adjusted by one.

Uncirculated Sets

			£
US01–**1982**	Uncirculated (specimen) set in Royal Mint folder, 50p to ½p, new reverse type, including 20 pence (Issued: 205,000)..	(7)	9
US02–**1983**	'U.K.' £1 (4221) to ½p (Issued: 637,100)	(8)	15
US03–**1984**	'Scottish' £1 (4222) to ½p (Issued: 158,820)	(8)	15
US04–**1985**	'Welsh' £1 (4331) to 1p, new portrait of The Queen (Issued: 102,015)..........	(7)	15
US05–**1986**	'Commonwealth Games' £2 (4311) plus 'Northern Irish' £1 (4332) to 1p, (Issued: 167,224)...	(8)	18
US06–**1987**	'English' £1 (4333) to 1p, (Issued: 172,425)...	(7)	15
US07–**1988**	'Arms' £1 (4334) to 1p, (Issued: 134,067)..	(7)	15
US08–**1989**	'Scottish' £1 (4335) to 1p, (Issued: 77,569)	(7)	20
US09–**1989**	'Bill of Rights' and 'Claim of Right' £2s (4312 and 4313) in Royal Mint folder (Issued: not known)	(2)	25
US10–**1990**	'Welsh' £1 (4331) to 1p plus new smaller 5p, (Issued: 102,606)...................	(8)	20
US11–**1991**	'Northern Irish' £1 (4332) to 1p, (Issued: 74,975)	(7)	20
US12–**1992**	'English' £1 (4333), 'European Community' 50p (4352) and 'Britannia' 50p, 20p to 1p plus new smaller 10p (Issued: 78,421)..	(9)	25
US13-**1992**	'European Community' 50p (4352) and 'Britannia' 50p (4351) in presentation folder previously listed as 4352A...	(2)	20
US14–**1993**	'UK' £1 (4336), 'European Community' 50p (4352) to 1p ((Issued: 56,945)	(8)	25
US15–**1994**	'Bank of England' £2 (4314), 'Scottish' £1 (4337) and 'D-Day' 50p (4353) to 1p, (Issued: 177,971)...	(8)	15
US16–**1995**	'Peace' £2 (4315) and 'Welsh' £1 (4338) to 1p (Issued: 105, 647).................	(8)	15
US17–**1996**	'Football' £2 (4317) and 'Northern Irish' £1 (4339) to 1p (Issued: 86,501)...	(8)	15
US18–**1997**	'Bimetallic' £2 (4318), 'English' £1 (4340) to 1p plus new smaller 50p (Issued: 109,557)...	(9)	15
US19–**1998**	'Bimetallic' £2 (4570), 'UK' £1 (4590) and 'EU' 50 pence (4611) to1 pence (Issued: 96,192)...	(9)	25
US20–**1998**	'EU' and 'Britannia' 50 pence (4611 and 4610) in Royal Mint folder............	(2)	6
US21–**1999**	'Bimetallic' 'Rugby' £2 (4571), 'Scottish' £1 (4591) to 1p (Issued: 136,696)	(8)	18
US22–**2000**	'Bimetallic' £2 (4570), 'Welsh' £1 (4592) to 1p plus 'Library' 50 pence (4613) (Issued: 117,750)	(9)	18
US23–**2001**	'Bimetallic' £2 (4570), 'Bimetallic' 'Marconi' £2 (4572), 'Irish' £1 (4594) to 1p (Issued: 57,741)	(9)	18

			£
US24–**2002**	'Bimetallic' £2 (4570), 'English' £1 (4594) to 1p (Issued: 60,539)	(8)	18
US25–**2002**	'Bimetallic' £2 Commonwealth Games set of four (4573, 4574, 4575 and 4576) (Issued: 47,895)	(4)	45
US26–**2003**	Bimetallic 'DNA' £2 (4577), 'Bimetallic' £2 (4570), 'UK' £1 (4590), 'Suffragette' 50 pence (4614) and 'Britannia' 50 pence (4610) to 1p. (Issued: 62,741)	(10)	28
US27–**2004**	'Bimetallic' 'Penydarren engine' £2 (4578), 'Bimetallic' £2 (4570), 'Forth Rail Bridge' £1 (4595), 'Sub four-minute mile' 50 pence (4615) and 'Britannia' 50 pence (4610) to1p. (Issued: 46,032)	(10)	28
US28–**2004**	'Bimetallic' 'Penydarren engine' £2 (4578), 'Forth Rail Bridge' £1(4595), 'Sub four-minute mile' 50 pence (4615). (Issued: 14,391)	(3)	10
US29–**2005**	'Bimetallic' 'Gunpowder Plot' £2 (4579), 'Bimetallic' £2 (4570), 'Menai Straits Bridge' £1 (4596), 'Samuel Johnson's Dictionary' 50 pence (4616) and 'Britannia' 50 pence (4610) to 1p. (Issued: 51,776)	(10)	20
US30–**2005**	'Bimetallic' 'Gunpowder Plot' £2 (4579), 'Menai Straits Bridge' £1 (4596), 'Samuel Johnson's Dictionary' 50 pence (4616)	(3)	10
US31–**2005**	'Trafalgar' £5, struck in c/n (4559) and 'Nelson' £5 struck in c/n (4560)	(2)	25
US32–**2006**	'Bimetallic' 'Isambard Brunel' £2 (4581), 'Bimetallic' 'Paddington Station' £2 (4582), 'MacNeill's Egyptian Arch' £1 (4597), 'Victoria Cross' 50 pence (4617), 'Wounded soldier' 50 pence (4618) to 1p (Issued: 74,231)	(10)	28
US33–**2006**	'Bimetallic' 'Isambard Brunel' £2 (4581), 'Bimetallic' 'Paddington Station' £2 (4582)	(2)	10
US34–**2006**	'Victoria Cross' 50 pence (4617), 'Wounded soldier' 50 pence (4618)	(2)	8
US35–**2007**	'Bimetallic' 'Act of Union' £2 (4583), 'Bimetallic' 'Abolition of Slave Trade' £2 (4584), 'Gateshead Millennium Bridge' £1 (4598), 'Scouting Movement' 50 pence, to 1p (Issued: 91,878)	(9)	24
US36–**2008**	'Bimetallic' 'London Olympics Centenary' £2 (4951), 'Bimetallic' £2 (4570), 'UK' £1 (4590), 'Britannia' 50 pence (4610), to 1p (Issued: 79,118)	(9)	20
US37–**2008**	'Emblems of Britain', 'UK' £1 (4590), 'Britannia' 50 pence (4610), and 20 pence to 1 p (Issued: 57,126)	(7)	12
US38–**2008**	'The Royal Shield of Arms', 'Royal Shield' £1 (4604) to1p (4611, 4631, 4651, 4671, 4691, 4711) (Issued: 100,000)	(7)	16
US39–**2009**	'Bimetallic' 'Charles Darwin' £2 (4586), Bimetallic 'Robert Burns' £2 (4585) 'Bimetallic'£2 (4570), 'Royal Shield' £1 (4604), 50 pence 'Kew Gardens' (4621) 50 pence (4620), 20 pence (4631), 10 pence (4651), 5 pence (4671), 2 pence (4691) and 1 pence (4711) (Edition: 100,000)	(11)	22
US40- **2009**	'Bimetallic'£2 (4570), 'Royal Shield' £1 (4604), 50 pence 'Kew Gardens' (4621) 50 pence (4620), 20 pence (4631), 10 pence (4651), 5 pence (4671), 2 pence (4691) and 1 pence (4711)	(8)	15
US41- **2009**	'Royal Shield' £1 (4604), 50 pence (4620), 20 pence (4631), 10 pence (4651), 5 pence (4671), 2 pence (4691) and 1 pence (4711)	(7)	15
US42–**2010**	'Bimetallic 'Florence Nightingale' £2 (4587), 'Bimetallic'£2 (4570), 'London' £1 (4605), 'Belfast' £1 (4606), 'Royal Shield '£1(4604), 50 pence 'Girl Guiding' (4626), 50 pence (4620), 20 pence (4631), 10 pence (4651), 5 pence (4671), 2 pence (4691) and 1 pence (4711) (Edition: 50,000)	(12)	25
US43–**2010**	'Bimetallic'£2 (4570), 'Royal Shield' £1 (4604), 50 pence (4620), 20 pence (4631), 10 pence (4651), 5 pence (4671), 2 pence (4691) and 1 pence (4711)	(8)	15
US44–**2010**	'London' £1 (4605) and 'Belfast' £1 (4606) (Edition: 10,000)	(2)	13
US45–**2011**	'Bimetallic' 'Mary Rose' £2 (4588), 'Bimetallic' King James Bible'£2 (4589), 'Bimetallic' £2 (4570) 'Edinburgh' £1 (4607), 'Cardiff' £1 (4608), 'Royal Shield '£1(4604), 50 pence,' WWF' (4627), 50 pence to 1 pence (4620, 4631, 4651, 4671, 4691 and 4711)	(13)	26

			£
US46–**2011**	'Bimetallic'£2 (4570), 'Royal Shield' £1 (4604), 50 pence to 1 pence (4620, 4631, 4651, 4671, 4691 4711)	(8)	21
US47–**2011**	'Edinburgh' £1 (4607) and 'Cardiff' £1 (4608) (Edition: 10,000)	(2)	14
US48–**2012**	Diamond Jubilee £5, struck in c/n (4569), 'Bimetallic' 'Charles Dickens' £2 (4730), 'Bimetallic' £2 (4570) 'Royal Shield' £1 (4604), 50 pence to 1 pence (4620, 4631, 4652, 4672, 4691 and 4711)......................................	(10)	39
US49–**2012**	'Bimetallic' £2 (4570) 'Royal Shield '£1(4604), 50 pence to 1 pence (4620, 4631, 4652, 4672, 4691 and 4711)	(8)	21
US50–**2013**	Coronation £5, struck in c/n (4751), 'Bimetallic' 'Guinea' £2 (4731), 'Bimetallic' 'Roundel' £2 (4732), 'Bimetallic' 'Train' £2 (4733), 'Bimetallic' £2 (4570) 'Royal Shield' £1 (4604), 'England' £1 (4720), 'Wales' £1 (4721), 50 pence 'Ironside' (4628), 50 pence to 1 pence (4620, 4631, 4652, 4672, 4691 and 4711)	(15)	50
US51–**2013**	'Bimetallic' £2 (4570) 'Royal Shield '£1 (4604), 50 pence to 1 pence (4620, 4631, 4652, 4672, 4691 and 4711)	(8)	£25
US52–**2014**	Queen Anne £5, struck in c/n (4758), 'Bimetallic' 'Trinity House' £2 (4734), 'Bimetallic' 'World War I' £2 (4735), 'Bimetallic' £2 (4570) 'Royal Shield' £1 (4604), 'Northern Ireland' £1 (4722), 'Scotland' £1(4723.), 50 pence 'Commonwealth Games' (4630), 50 pence to 1 pence (4620, 4636, 4652, 4672, 4691 and 4711)	(14)	£50
US53–**2014**	'Bimetallic' £2 (4570) 'Royal Shield '£1(4604), 50 pence to 1 pence (4620, 4631, 4652, 4672, 4691 and 4711	(8)	£25

Proof Sets

PS21–**1971**	Decimal coinage set, 50 new pence 'Britannia' to $1/2$ new pence, in sealed plastic case with card wrapper (Issued: 350,000).................................	(6)	18
PS22–**1972**	Proof 'Silver Wedding' Crown struck in c/n (4226) plus 50p to ½p (Issued: 150,000)...	(7)	20
PS23–**1973**	'EEC' 50p (4224) plus 10p to ½p, (Issued: 100,000)...............................	(6)	15
PS24–**1974**	'Britannia' 50p to ½p, as 1971 (Issued: 100,000).................................	(6)	15
PS25–**1975**	'Britannia' 50p to ½p (as 1974), (Issued: 100,000)	(6)	12
PS26–**1976**	'Britannia' 50p to ½p, as 1975, (Issued: 100,000)................................	(6)	12
PS27–**1977**	Proof 'Silver Jubilee' Crown struck in c/n (4227) plus 50p to ½p, (Issued: 193,000)	(7)	12
PS28–**1978**	'Britannia' 50p to ½p, as 1976, (Issued: 86,100)................................	(6)	12
PS29–**1979**	'Britannia' 50p to ½p, as 1978, (Issued: 81,000)	(6)	12
PS30–**1980**	'Britannia' 50p to ½p, as 1979, (Issued: 143,000).............................	(6)	15
PS31–**1981**	'Britannia' 50p to ½p, as 1980, (Issued: 100,300).............................	(6)	15
PS32–**1982**	'Britannia' 50p to ½p including 20 pence (Issued: 106,800)	(7)	15
PS33–**1983**	'U.K.' £1 (4221) to ½p in new packaging (Issued: 107,800)..................	(8)	20
PS34–**1984**	'Scottish' £1 (4222) to ½p, (Issued: 106,520)...................................	(8)	20
PS35–**1985**	'Welsh' £1 (4331) to 1p, (Issued: 102,015)......................................	(7)	20
PS36–**1985**	As last but packed in deluxe red leather case (Included above).....................	(7)	20
PS37–**1986**	'Commonwealth Games' £2 (4311) plus 'Northern Irish' £1 (4332) to 1p, (Issued: 104,597)...	(8)	20
PS38–**1986**	As last but packed in deluxe red leather case (Included above)....................	(8)	23
PS39–**1987**	'English' £1 (4333) to 1p, (Issued: 88,659)......................................	(7)	20
PS40–**1987**	As last but packed in deluxe leather case (Included above)...........................	(7)	23
PS41–**1988**	'Arms' £1 (4334) to 1p, (Issued: 79,314)...	(7)	25
PS42–**1988**	As last but packed in deluxe leather case (Included above)...........................	(7)	29
PS43–**1989**	'Bill of Rights' and 'Claim of Right' £2s (4312 and 4313), 'Scottish' £1 (4335) to 1p, (Issued: 85,704)..	(9)	30
PS44–**1989**	As last but packed in red leather case, (Included above)	(9)	35

£

			£
PS45–**1990**	'Welsh' £1 (4331) to 1p plus new smaller 5p, (Issued: 79,052)......	(8)	27
PS46–**1990**	As last but packed in red leather case (Included above)	(8)	32
PS47–**1991**	'Northern Irish' £1 (4332) to 1p, (Issued: 55,144)	(7)	27
PS48–**1991**	As last but packed in red leather case (Included above)	(7)	33
PS49–**1992**	'English' £1 (4333), 'European community' 50p (4352) and 'Britannia' 50p,		
	20p to 1p plus new smaller 10p, (Issued: 44,337)...........................	(9)	28
PS50–**1992**	As last but packed in red leather case (Issued: 17,989)	(9)	33
PS51–**1993**	Proof 'Coronation Anniversary' £5 struck in c/n (4302), 'U.K.' £1 (4336), 50p		
	to 1p, (Issued: 43,509)...	(8)	30
PS52–**1993**	As last but packed in red leather case (Issued: 22,571)	(8)	35
PS53–**1994**	'Bank' £2 (4314), 'Scottish' £1 (4337), 'D-Day' 50p (4353) to 1p, (Issued: 44,643)	(8)	30
PS54–**1994**	As last but packed in red leather case (Issued: 22,078)....................	(8)	35
PS55–**1995**	'Peace' £2 (4315), 'Welsh' £1 (4338) to 1p, (Issued: 42,842)............	(8)	32
PS56–**1995**	As last but packed in red leather case (Issued: 17,797)....................	(8)	35
PS57–**1996**	Proof '70th Birthday' £5 struck in c/n (4303), 'Football' £2 (4317), 'Northern		
	Irish' £1 (4339) to 1p, (Issued: 46,295)..	(9)	32
PS58–**1996**	As last but packed in red leather case (Issued: 21,286)...................	(9)	37
PS59–**1997**	Proof 'Golden Wedding' £5 struck in c/n (4304), 'Bimetallic' £2 (4318),		
	'English' £1 (4340) to 1p plus new smaller 50p (Issued: 48,761)	(10)	33
PS60–**1997**	As last but packed in red leather case (Issued: 31,987).....................	(10)	40
PS61–**1998**	Proof 'Prince of Wales 50th Birthday'£5 struck in c/n (4550), 'Bimetallic' £2		
	(4570), 'UK'. £1 (4590), 'EU' 50 pence (4611) to 1p. (Issued: 36,907)........	(10)	33
PS62–**1998**	As last, but packed in red leather case (Issued: 26,763)......................	(10)	40
PS63–**1999**	Proof 'Diana, Princess of Wales' £5 struck in c/n (4551), 'Bimetallic' 'Rugby'		
	£2 (4571), 'Scottish' £1 (4591) to 1p. (Issued: 40,317)	(9)	34
PS64–**1999**	As last, but packed in red leather case. (Issued: 39,827)...................	(9)	40
PS65–**2000**	Proof 'Millennium' £5 struck in c/n (4552), 'Bimetallic' £2 (4570), 'Welsh' £1		
	(4592), 'Library' 50 pence (4613) and 'Britannia' 50 pence (4610) to 1p. Standard		
	Set, (Issued: 41,379)..	(10)	30
PS66–**2000**	As last, but Deluxe set (Issued: 21,573 above)	(10)	30
PS67–**2000**	As last, but Executive set (Issued: 9,517)	(10)	60
PS68–**2001**	Proof 'Victoria' £5 struck in c/n (4554), 'Bimetallic' £2 (4570), 'Bimetallic'		
	'Marconi' £2 (4572), 'Irish' £1 (4593) to 1p. Standard Set. (Issued: 28,244).	(10)	34
PS69–**2001**	As last, but Gift Set (Issued: 1,351)	(10)	30
PS70–**2001**	As last, but packed in red leather case (Issued: 16,022)....................	(10)	48
PS71–**2001**	As last, but Executive Set (Issued: 3,755).....................................	(10)	60
PS72–**2002**	Proof 'Golden Jubilee' £5 struck in c/n (4555), 'Bimetallic' £2 (4570),		
	'English' £1 (4594) to 1p. Standard set. (Issued: 30,884).................	(9)	32
PS73–**2002**	As last, but Gift Set (Issued: 1,544)	(9)	30
PS74–**2002**	As last, but packed in red leather case (Issued: 23,342)....................	(9)	46
PS75–**2002**	As last, but Executive Set (Issued: 5,000).....................................	(9)	70
PS76–**2002**	'Bimetallic' 'Commonwealth Games'£2 (4573, 4574, 4575 and 4576)		
	(Issued: 3,358)..	(4)	36
PS77–**2002**	As last, but Display Set (Issued: 673)	(4)	33
PS78–**2003**	Proof 'Coronation'£5 struck in c/n (4557), 'Bimetallic' 'DNA' £2 (4577),		
	'Bimetallic' £2 (4570), 'UK' £1 (4590), 'Suffragette' 50 pence (4614) and		
	'Britannia' 50 pence (4610) to 1p. Standard set. (Issued: 23,650)	(11)	34
PS79–**2003**	As last, but packed in red leather case (Issued: 14,863)...................	(11)	47
PS80–**2003**	As last, but Executive Set (Issued: 5,000).....................................	(11)	70
PS81–**2004**	'Bimetallic' 'Penydarren engine' £2 (4578), 'Bimetallic' £2 (4570), 'Forth Rail		
	Bridge' £1 (4595), 'Sub four-minute mile' 50 pence (4615) and 'Britannia'		
	50 pence (4610) to 1p. Standard set. (Issued: 17,951)	(10)	35

£

PS82–**2004**	As last, but packed in red leather case (Issued: 12,968).....................................	(10)	45
PS83–**2004**	As last, but Executive Set (Issued: 4,101)...	(10)	65
PS84–**2005**	Proof 'Trafalgar'£5 struck in c/n (4559), Proof 'Nelson'£5 struck in c/n (4560) 'Bimetallic' 'Gunpowder Plot' £2 (4579), 'Bimetallic' £2 (4570), 'Menai Straits Bridge' £1 (4596), 'Samuel Johnson's Dictionary' 50 pence (4616) and 'Britannia' 50 pence (4610) to 1p. (Issued: 21,374).......................................	(12)	40
PS85–**2005**	As last, but packed in red leather case (Issued: 14,899)................................	(12)	50
PS86–**2005**	As last, but Executive Set (Issued: 4,290)..	(12)	75
PS87–**2006**	Proof '80th Birthday'£5 struck in c/n (4561), 'Bimetallic' 'Isambard Brunel' £2 (4581), 'Bimetallic' 'Paddington Station' £2 (4582), 'Bimetallic' £2 (4570), 'MacNeill's Egyptian Arch' £1 (4597), 'Victoria Cross' 50 pence (4617), 'Wounded soldier' 50 pence (4618) and 'Britannia' 50 pence (4610) to 1p (Issued: 17,689)...	(13)	42
PS88 –**2006**	As last, but packed in red leather case (Issued: 15,000)................................	(13)	50
PS89–**2006**	As last, but Executive Set (Issued: 5,000)..	(13)	78
PS90 –**2007**	Proof 'Diamond Wedding'£5 struck in c/n (4562), 'Bimetallic' 'Act of Union' £2 (4583), 'Bimetallic' 'Abolition of Slave Trade' £2 (4584), 'Gateshead Millennium Bridge' £1 (4598), 'Scouting Movement' 50 pence (4619), and 'Britannia' 50p (4610) to 1p (Issued: 18,215)..	(12)	40
PS91 –**2007**	As last, but packed in red leather case (Issued: 15,000)................................	(12)	50
PS92 –**2007**	As last, but Executive Set (Issued: 5,000)..	(12)	78
PS93 –**2008**	Proof 'Prince Charles 60th Birthday' £5 struck in c/n (4564), Proof 'Elizabeth I Anniversary' struck in c/n (4563), 'Bimetallic' 'London Olympics Centenary' £2 (4951), 'Bimetallic' £2 (4570) 'UK' £1 (4590), and 'Britannia' 50p (4610) to 1p (Issued: 17,719)...	(11)	40
PS94 – **2008**	As last, but packed in black leather case (Issued: 13,614).............................	(11)	50
PS95 – **2008**	As last, but Executive Set (Issued: 5,000)..	(11)	80
PS96 – **2008**	'The Royal Shield of Arms', 'Royal Shield' £1 (4604) to 1p (4611, 4631, 4651, 4671, 4691, 4711) (Issued: 20,000)...	(7)	45
PS97 – **2009**	Proof 'Henry VIII' £5 struck in c/n (4565), 'Bimetallic' 'Charles Darwin' £2 (4586), 'Bimetallic' 'Robert Burns' £2 (4585) 'Bimetallic' £2 (4570), 'Royal Shield' £1 (4604), 'Kew Gardens' 50 pence (4621) 50 pence (4620), 20 pence (4631), 10 pence (4651), 5 pence (4671), 2 pence (4691) and 1 pence (4711) (Edition: 20,000)	(12)	40
PS98 – **2009**	As last, but packed in black leather case (Edition: 15,000)	(12)	50
PS99 – **2009**	As last, but Executive Set (Edition: 5,000).......................................	(12)	80
PS100–**2009**	Set of sixteen 50 pence reverse designs marking the 40th Anniversary of the introduction of the 50 pence denomination (4610- 4625) (Edition: 5,000)	(16)	195
PS101–**2010**	Proof 'Restoration of the Monarchy' £5 struck in c/n (4566), 'Bimetallic' 'Florence Nightingale' £2 (4587), 'Bimetallic'£2 (4570), 'London' £1 (4605), 'Belfast' £1 (4606), Royal Shield £1 (4604), 'Girl Guiding' 50 pence (4626), and 50 pence to 1 pence (4620, 4631, 4651, 4671, 4691and 4711) (Edition: 20,000)	(13)	40
PS102–**2010**	As last, but packed in black leather case (Edition: 15,000)	(13)	50
PS103–**2010**	As last, but Executive Set (Edition: 5,000)	(13)	80
PS104–**2011**	Proof 'Prince Philip 90th Birthday' £5 struck in c/n (4568),'Bimetallic' 'Mary Rose' £2 (4588), 'Bimetallic' King James Bible'£2 (4589), 'Bimetallic' £2 (4570) 'Edinburgh' £1 (4607), 'Cardiff' £1 (4608), 'Royal Shield '£1(4604), 50 pence, 'WWF' (4627), 50 pence to 1 pence (4620, 4631, 4651, 4671, 4691, and 4711) (Edition: 20,000)...	(14)	45
PS105–**2011**	As last, but packed in black leather case (Edition: 15,000)........................	(14)	52
PS106–**2011**	As last, but Executive Set (Edition: 5,000)..	(14)	82

£

PS107–**2012** Diamond Jubilee £5, struck in c/n (4569), 'Bimetallic' 'Charles Dickens' £2
(4730), 'Bimetallic' £2 (4570) 'Royal Shield '£1(4604), 50 pence to 1 pence
(4620, 4631, 4652, 4672, 4691 and 4711) (Edition: 30,000).......... (10)   55

PS108–**2012** Premium Proof set, Proof Diamond Jubilee £5, struck in c/n (4569),
'Bimetallic' 'Charles Dickens' £2 (4730), 'Bimetallic' £2 (4570) 'Royal Shield
'£1(4604), 50 pence to 1 pence (4620, 4631, 4652, 4672, 4691, 4711)
and Mint medal (Edition:.3,500).. (10)   99

PS109–**2013** Premium Proof set, Coronation £5, struck in c/n (4751), 'Bimetallic'
'Guinea' £2 (4731) 'Bimetallic' 'Roundel' £2 (4732), 'Bimetallic' 'Train' £2
(4733),'Bimetallic' £2 (4570) 'Royal Shield' £1 (4604), 'England' £1 (4720),
'Wales' £1(4721), 50 pence 'Ironside' (4628), 50 pence to 1 pence (4620,
4631, 4652, 4672, 4691 and 4711) (Edition:4,000)...................... (15) 150

PS109–**2013** Collector Proof set, Coronation £5, struck in c/n (4751), 'Bimetallic' 'Guinea'
£2 (4731) 'Bimetallic' 'Roundel' £2 (4732), 'Bimetallic' 'Train' £2 (4733),
'Bimetallic' £2 (4570) 'Royal Shield' £1 (4604), 'England' £1 (4720), 'Wales'
£1 (4721), 50 pence 'Ironside' (4628), 50 pence to 1 pence (4620, 4631, 4652,
4672, 4691 and 4711) (Edition:30,000 .... (15) 110

PS111–**2013** Commemorative Proof set, Coronation £5, struck in c/n (4751), 'Bimetallic'
'Guinea' £2 (4731) 'Bimetallic' 'Roundel' £2 (4732), 'Bimetallic' 'Train'£2
(4733), 'England' £1 (4720), 'Wales' £1(4721)and 50 pence 'Ironside' (4628)
(Edition: 10,000) .... (7)   65

PS112–**2014** Premium Proof set, Queen Anne £5, struck in c/n (4758), 'Bimetallic'
'Trinity House' £2 (4734), 'Bimetallic' 'World War I' £2 (4735), 'Bimetallic'
£2 (4570) 'Royal Shield' £1 (4604), 'Northern Ireland' £1 (4722), 'Scotland'
£1(4723.), 50 pence 'Commonwealth Games' (4630), 50 pence to 1 pence
(4620, 4636, 4652, 4672, 4691 and 4711) (Edition: 4,500).......... (14)£155

PS113–**2014** Collector Proof set, Queen Anne £5, struck in c/n (4758), 'Bimetallic'
'Trinity House' £2 (4734), 'Bimetallic' 'World War I' £2 (4735), 'Bimetallic'
£2 (4570) 'Royal Shield' £1 (4604), 'Northern Ireland' £1 (4722), 'Scotland'
£1 (4723.), 50 pence 'Commonwealth Games' (4630), 50 pence to 1 pence
(4620, 4636, 4652, 4672, 4691 and 4711) (Edition: 30,000).......... (14)£110

PS114–**2014** Commemorative Proof set, Queen Anne £5, struck in c/n (4758), 'Bimetallic'
'Trinity House' £2 (4734), Bimetallic' 'World War I' £2 (4735), 'Northern
Ireland' £1 (4722), 'Scotland' £1(4723.), and 50 pence 'Commonwealth
Games' (4630), (Edition: 7,500) .... (6)   £65

Silver Maundy Sets   *FDC* £   *FDC* £

4211   Maundy Set (4p, 3p, 2p and 1p). Uniform dates. Types as 4131

1971 *Tewkesbury Abbey*	225	1989 *Birmingham Cathedral*	200
1972 *York Minster*	200	1990 *Newcastle Cathedral*	200
1973 *Westminster Abbey*	200	1991 *Westminster Abbey*	225
1974 *Salisbury Cathedral*	200	1992 *Chester Cathedral*	200
1975 *Peterborough Cathedral*	200	1993 *Wells Cathedral*	200
1976 *Hereford Cathedral*	200	1994 *Truro Cathedral*	200
1977 *Westminster Abbey*	200	1995 *Coventry Cathedral*	200
1978 *Carlisle Cathedral*	200	1996 *Norwich Cathedral*	200
1979 *Winchester Cathedral*	200	1997 *Bradford Cathedral*	200
1980 *Worcester Cathedral*	200	1998 *Portsmouth Cathedral*	200
1981 *Westminster Abbey*	225	1999 *Bristol Cathedral*	200
1982 *St. Davidís Cathedral*	200	2000 *Lincoln Cathedral*	200

1983 *Exeter Cathedral*	200	2001 *Westminster Abbey*	225
1984 *Southwell Minster*	200	2002 *Canterbury Cathedral*	200
1985 *Ripon Cathedral*	200	2002 *Proof in gold from set* *(see PCGS1)	1850
1986 *Chichester Cathedral*	200	2003 *Gloucester Cathedral*	200
1987 *Ely Cathedral*	200	2004 *Liverpool Cathedral*	200
1988 *Lichfield Cathedral*	200	2005 *Wakefield Cathedral*	200

£

4212 — fourpence, 1971-2010...*from* 50
4213 — threepence, 1971-2010...*from* 50
4214 — twopence, 1971-2010..*from* 50
4215 — penny, 1971-2010...*from* 75

The place of distribution is shown after each date.

Silver Sets
£

PSS01–**1989**	'Bill of Rights' and 'Claim of Right' £2s (4312 and 4313), Silver piedfort proofs (Issued: 10,000)	(2)	85
PSS02–**1989**	As last but Silver proofs (Not known)	(2)	65
PSS03–**1990**	2 x 5p Silver proofs (4371 and 4372), (Issued: 35,000)	(2)	30
PSS04–**1992**	2 x 10p Silver proofs (4366 and 4367), (Not known)…	(2)	34
PSS05–**1996**	25th Anniversary of Decimal Currency (4339, 4351, 4361, 4367, 4372, 4386, 4391) in Silver proof (Edition: 15,000)	(7)	125
PSS06–**1997**	2 x 50p silver proofs (4351 and 4354) (Issued: 10,304)	(2)	45
PSS07–**1998**	'EU' and 'NHS' Silver proofs (4611 and 4612)	(2)	60
PSS08–**2000**	'Millennium' £5, 'Bimetallic' £2, 'Welsh' £1, 50p to 1p, and Maundy coins, 4p-1p, in silver proof (4552, 4570, 4592, 4610, 4630, 4650, 4670, 4212-4215) (Issued: 13,180)	(13)	275
PSS09–**2002**	'Commonwealth Games' 'Bimetallic' £2 (4573, 4574, 4575 and 4576) in silver (Issued: 2,553)	(4)	140
PSS10–**2002**	As above with the addition of colour and piedfort in silver. (4573A, 4574A, 4575A and 4576A) (Issued: 3,497)	(4)	240
PSS11–**MD**	'Golden Jubilee' £5 (4555) and 'Coronation' £5 (4557) silver proofs	(2)	110
PSS12–**2003**	'Coronation' £5 (4557), 'Britannia' £2 (4503), 'Bimetallic' 'DNA' £2 (4577), 'UK' £1 (4590) and 'Suffragette' 50 pence (4614) silver proofs (Edition:)	(5)	165
PSS13–**2004**	'Entente Cordiale' £5 (4558), 'Britannia' £2 (4500), 'Bimetallic' 'Penydarren engine' £2 (4578) 'Forth Rail Bridge' £1 (4595) and 'Sub four-minute mile' 50 pence (4615) silver proofs (Edition:)	(5)	165
PSS14–**2004**	'Bimetallic' 'Penydarren engine' £2 (4578), 'Forth Rail Bridge' £1 (4595), 'Sub four-minute mile' 50 pence (4615) Silver piedfort proofs	(3)	145

£

PSS15–**2005**	'Bimetallic' 'Gunpowder Plot' £2 (4579), Bimetallic' 'World War II' £2 (4580), 'Menai Straits Bridge' £1 (4596), 'Samuel Johnson's Dictionary' 50 pence Silver piedfort proofs	(4)	190
PSS16–**2005**	'Trafalgar' £5 (4559) and 'Nelson' £5 (4560) silver piedfort proofs, (Issued: 2,818)	(2)	175
PSS17–**2006**	'H M The Queen's 80th Birthday' £5, 'Bimetallic' £2, 'Northern Ireland' £1, 50p to 1p, (4561, 4570, 4597, 4610, 4630, 4650, 4670, and Maundy Coins, 4p – 1p, in silver proof, (4212 – 4215) (Edition: 8,000)	(13)	275
PSS18–**2006**	'Bimetallic' 'Isambard Brunel' £2 (4581) and 'Bimetallic' 'Paddington Station' £2 (4582) silver proofs (Edition: taken from individual coin limits)	(2)	70
PSS19–**2006**	As last but silver piedforts (Edition: 5,000)	(2)	130
PSS20–**2006**	'Victoria Cross' 50 pence (4617) and 'Wounded soldier' 50 pence (4618) silver proofs (Edition: taken from individual coin limits)	(2)	65
PSS21–**2006**	As last but silver piedforts (Edition: 5,000)	(2)	115

£

			£
PSS22–**2006**	'80th Birthday' £5 (4561), 'Bimetallic' 'Isambard Brunel' £2 (4581) and 'Bimetallic' 'Paddington Station' £2 (4582), 'MacNeill's Egyptian Arch' £1 (4597), 'Victoria Cross' 50 pence (4617), 'Wounded soldier' 50 pence (4618) silver piedforts (Edition: taken from individual coin limits)............................	(6)	325
PSS23–**2007**	'Diamond Wedding' £5, Britannia £2, 'Bimetallic' 'Act of Union' £2, 'Bimetallic' 'Abolition of Slavery' £2, 'Millennium Bridge' £1 and 'Scout Movement' 50p in silver proof (4562, 4505, 4583, 4584, 4598 and 4619) (Edition: taken from individual coin limits)	(6)	200
PSS24–**2007**	'Diamond Wedding' £5, 'Bimetallic' 'Act of Union' £2, 'Bimetallic' 'Abolition of Slavery' £2, 'Millennium Bridge' £1 and 'Scout Movement' 50p in silver piedfort (4562, 4583, 4584, 4598 and 4619) (Edition: taken from individual coin limits	(5)	250
PSS25–**MD**	Set of four £1 coins 'Forth Rail Bridge' (4595), 'Menai Straits Bridge' (4596) 'MacNeill's Egyptian Arch' (4597) and 'Gateshead Millennium Bridge' (4598) in silver proof (Edition: taken from individual coin limits)	(4)	115
PSS26–**MD**	As above but in silver piedfort (Edition: 1,400 taken from individual coin limits)...	(4)	200
PSS27–**2008**	'Emblems of Britain', 'UK' £1 (4590), 'Britannia' 50 pence (4610), 20 pence to 1p silver proofs (Issued: 8,168)..	(7)	150
PSS28–**2008**	'The Royal Shield of Arms', 'Royal Shield' £1 (4604) to 1p (4611, 4631, 4651, 4671, 4691, 4711) silver proof (Issued: 10,000)	(7)	160
PSS29–**2008**	As above but silver piedforts (Issued: 3,000)...	(7)	295

£

			£
PSS30–**2008**	Set of 14 different £1 with selected gold plating to the reverse designs (4590 to 4603) (Edition: 15,000 collections)..	(14)	395
PSS31–**2008**	Set of 3 £1 Regional designs for Scotland with selected gold plating to the reverse designs (4591B, 4595C and 4599A) (Edition: 750, taken from above)	(3)	95
PSS32–**2008**	Set of 3 £1 Regional designs for Wales with selected gold plating to the reverse designs (4592B, 4596C and 4600A) (Edition: 750, taken from above)...........	(3)	95
PSS33–**2008**	Set of 3 £1 Regional designs for Northern Ireland with selected gold plating to the reverse designs (4593B, 4597C and 4601A) (Edition: 750, taken from above)	(3)	95
PSS34–**2008**	Set of 3 £1 Regional designs for England with selected gold plating to the reverse designs (4594B, 4598C and 4602A) (Edition: 750, taken from above)	(3)	95
PSS35–**2008**	'Prince Charles 60th Birthday' £5 (4563), 'Elizabeth I Anniversary' £5 (4564), Britannia £2 (4506), 'London Olympic Centenary' £2 (4951) and 'UK' £1 (4590) silver proofs (Edition: 5,000)..	(5)	180
PSS36–**2008**	'Prince Charles 60th Birthday' £5 (4563), 'Elizabeth I Anniversary' £5 (4564), 'London Olympic Centenary' £2 (4951) and 'Royal Shield' £1 (4604) silver piedforts (Edition: 3,000)	(4)	250
PSS37–**2009**	'Henry VIII" £5 (4565), 'Bimetallic' 'Charles Darwin' £2 (4586), Bimetallic 'Robert Burns' £2 (4585) 'Bimetallic' £2 (4570), 'Royal Shield' £1 (4604), 'Kew Gardens' 50 pence (4621), 50 pence (4620), 20 pence (4631), 10 pence (4651), 5 pence (4671), 2 pence (4691) and 1 pence (4711) silver proofs (Edition: 7,500...	(12)	270
PSS38–**2009**	'Henry VIII' £5 (4565), Britannia £2 (4501), 'Charles Darwin' £2 (4586), 'Robert Burns' £2 (4585), 'Royal Shield' £1 (4604) and 50 pence 'Kew Gardens' (4621) silver proofs (Edition: 1,500)..	(6)	200
PSS39–**2009**	'Henry VIII' £5 (4565), 'Charles Darwin' £2 (4586), 'Robert Burns' £2 (4585) and 50 pence 'Kew Gardens' (4621) silver piedforts (Edition: 2,500)	(4)	255
PSS40–**2009**	Set of sixteen 50 pence reverse designs marking 40th Anniversary of the introduction of the 50 pence denomination (4610- 4625) silver proofs (Edition: 2,500)	(16)	425

£

PSS41–**2010** 'Restoration of the Monarchy' £5 (4566), 'Bimetallic 'Florence Nightingale' £2 (4587), 'Bimetallic'£2 (4570), 'London' £1 (4605), 'Belfast' £1 (4606), Royal Shield £1 (4604), 'Girl Guiding' 50 pence (4626), and 50 pence to 1p (4620, 4631, 4651, 4671, 4691and 4711) silver proofs (Edition: 3,500) .... (13) 300

PSS42–**2010** 'Restoration of the Monarchy' £5 (4566), 'Bimetallic 'Florence Nightingale' £2 (4587), 'London' £1 (4605), 'Belfast' £1 (4606), and 'Girl Guiding' 50 pence (4626) silver proofs (Edition: 2,500) .... (5) 180

PSS43–**2010** 'Restoration of the Monarchy'£5 (4566), 'Bimetallic 'Florence Nightingale' £2 (4587), 'London' £1 (4605), 'Belfast' £1 (4606), and 'Girl Guiding' 50 pence (4626) silver piedforts (Edition: 2,500) .... (5) 300

PSS44-**2011** Proof 'Prince Philip 90th Birthday' £5 (4568), 'Bimetallic' 'Mary Rose' £2 (4588), 'Bimetallic' King James Bible'£2 (4589), 'Bimetallic' £2 (4570) 'Edinburgh' £1 (4607), 'Cardiff' £1 (4608), 'Royal Shield '£1(4604), 50 pence,' WWF' (4627), 50 pence to 1 pence (4620, 4631, 4651, 4671, 4691 and 4711) silver proofs (Edition: 2,500) .... (14) 450

PSS45-**2011** Proof 'Prince Philip 90th Birthday' £5 (4568), 'Bimetallic' 'Mary Rose' £2 (4588), 'Bimetallic' King James Bible'£2 (4590), 'Edinburgh' £1 (4607), 'Cardiff' £1 (4608), 50 pence,' WWF' (4627), silver proofs (Edition: 1,500) .... (6) 285

PSS46-**2011** Proof 'Prince Philip 90th Birthday' £5 (4568), 'Bimetallic' 'Mary Rose' £2 (4589), 'Bimetallic' King James Bible'£2 (4589), 'Edinburgh' £1 (4607), 'Cardiff' £1 (4608), 'WWF' (4627), silver piedforts (Edition: 2,000) .... (6) 455

PSS47–**2012** Proof Diamond Jubilee £5, (4569), 50 pence to 1 pence (4620, 4631, 4652, 4672, 4691 and 4711) silver proofs, (Edition: 995) .... (7) 395

PSS48–**2012** Proof Diamond Jubilee £5, (4569), 'Bimetallic' 'Charles Dickens' £2 (4730), 'Bimetallic' £2 (4570) 'Royal Shield '£1(4604), 50 pence to 1 pence (4620, 4631, 4652, 4672, 4691 and 4711) silver proofs, the £2s to 1 pence with selected gold plating (Edition: 2,012) .... (10) 490

PSS49–**MD** Proof Silver Wedding Crown, 25pence, Golden Wedding Crown, £5 and Diamond Wedding Crown, £5 (4226, 4304 and 4562) silver proofs (Edition: 250 taken from the original sales and obtained from the secondary market). (3) 150

PSS50–**2013** Proof 'Coronation' £5, (4751), 'Bimetallic' 'Guinea' £2 (4731) 'Bimetallic' 'Roundel' (4732), 'Bimetallic' 'Train' £2 (4733), 'Bimetallic' £2 (4570) 'Royal Shield' £1 (4604), 'England' £1 (4720), 'Wales' £1 (4721), 50 pence 'Ironside' (4628), 50 pence to 1 pence (4620, 4631, 4652, 4672, 4691 and 4711) silver proofs (Edition:2,013) .... (15) 600

PSS51–**2013** Proof 'Coronation' £5, (4751), 'Bimetallic' 'Guinea' £2 (4731) 'Bimetallic' 'Roundel' £2 (4732), 'Bimetallic' 'Train'£2 (4733), 'England' £1 (4720), 'Wales' £1 (4721) and 50 pence 'Ironside' (4628) silver piedfort (Edition: 2,013) .... (7) 650

PSS52–**2013** 'Bimetallic' 'Roundel' £2 (4732) and 'Bimetallic' 'Train'£2 (4733) silver proofs (Edition: 1,500) .... (2) 100

PSS53–**2013** Queen's Portrait set of £5 coins, (4754 – 4757) silver proofs (Edition: 5,000) .... (4) 400

PSS54–**2013** Queen's Portrait set of £5 coins, (4754 – 4757) silver piedfort (Edition: 2,700) . (4) 800

PSS55–**2013** Thirtieth Anniversary set of three £1 coins, (4590, 4603 and 4604) silver (Edition: 3,500) .... (3) 150

PSS56–**2014** Proof 'Queen Anne' £5, (4758), 'Bimetallic' 'Trinity House' £2 (4734), 'Bimetallic' 'World War I' £2 (4735), 'Bimetallic' £2 (4570) 'Royal Shield' £1 (4604), 'Northern Ireland' £1 (4722), 'Scotland' £1 (4723.), 50 pence 'Commonwealth Games' (4630), 50 pence to 1 pence (4620, 4636, 4652, 4672, 4691 and 4711) silver proofs (Edition: 2,014) .... (14) 560

£

PSS57–**2014** Proof 'Queen Anne' £5, (4758), 'Bimetallic' 'Trinity House' £2 (4734),
'Bimetallic' 'World War I' £2 (4735), 'Bimetallic' £2 (4570) 'Royal Shield'
£1 (4604), 'Northern Ireland' £1 (4722), 'Scotland' £1 (4723.), and 50 pence
'Commonwealth Games' (4630), silver proofs (Edition: 1,000)................... (6)   295

PSS58–**2014** Proof 'Queen Anne' £5, (4758), 'Bimetallic' 'Trinity House' £2 (4734),
'Bimetallic' 'World War I' £2 (4735), 'Bimetallic' £2 (4570) 'Royal Shield'
£1 (4604), 'Northern Ireland' £1 (4722), 'Scotland' £1 (4723.), and 50 pence
'Commonwealth Games' (4630), silver piedforts (Edition: 2,014)............... (6)   570

PSS59–**2014** Celebrating British Landmarks. Set of four £5, (4760 – 4763), silver proofs
(Edition: 3,500) .... (4)   360

PSS60–**2014** World War 1. Set of six £5, (4764 – 4769), silver proofs (Edition: 1,914) .... (6)   450

Britannia Silver Proof Sets

PBS01–**1997** £2 – 20 pence (4300, 4300A, 4300B, 4300C) (Issued: 11,832)..................... (4)   175
PBS02–**1998** £2 – 20 pence (4500, 4510, 4520, 4530) (Issued: 3,044)................................ (4)   160
PBS03–**2001** £2 – 20 pence (4502, 4511, 4521, 4531) (Issued: 4,596)................................ (4)   150
PBS04–**2003** £2 – 20 pence (4503, 4512, 4522, 4532) (Issued: 3,669)................................ (4)   150
PBS05–**MD**   Britannia set of four different £2 designs, 1999- 2003 (4500, 4501,4502, 4503)
(Edition: 5,000) .... (4)   160
PBS06–**2005** Britannia proofs, £2 – 20 pence (4504, 4513, 4523, 4533) (Issued: 2,360)..... (4)   150
PBS07–**2006** Britannia set of five different £2 designs with selected gold Plating of obverse
and reverse (4500A, 4501A, 4502A, 4503A, 4504A) (Issued: 3,000)............. (5)   350
PBS08–**2007** Britannia proofs, £2 - 20 pence, (4505, 4514, 4524, 4534) (Issued: 2,500)..... (4)   150
PBS09–**2007** Britannia set of six different proof £1 designs with satin finish on reverse
(4510A, 4511A, 4512A, 4513A, 4514A, 4515) (Issued: 2,000) .... (6)   225
PBS10–**2008** Britannia proofs, £2 – 20p (4506, 4516, 4525, 4535) (Issued: 2,500) .... (4)   150
PBS11–**2009** Britannia proofs, £2 – 20p (4501, 4517, 4526, 4536) (Issued: 2,500) .... (4)   150
PBS12–**2010** Britannia proofs, £2 – 20p (4502, 4518, 4527, 4537) (Edition: 3,500)............ (4)   150
PBS13–**2011** Britannia proofs, £2 – 20p (4508, 4519, 4528, 45387) (Edition: 3,500) .... (4)   195
PBS14–**2012** Britannia proofs, £2 – 20p, (As PB02) (Edition: 2,600)............................... (4)   195
PBS15–**2012** Britannia £1 proofs, set of nine different reverse designs (4510 to 4514, and
4516 to 4519) (Edition: 1,612 sets) .... (9)   400
PBS16–**2013** Britannia proofs, £2 – 10p, (0.999 silver) (4509,4560,4529,4539 and 4550)
(Edition: 4,650) .... (5)   450
PBS17–**2013** Britannia proofs, 20p and 10p (0.999 silver) (4539 and 4550)................... (2)   39
PBS18–**2014** Britannia proofs, £2 – 5p, (0.999 silver) (4509, 4701, 4529, 4539 and 4550)
(Edition: 1,750) .... (6)   200
PBS19–**2014** Britannia proofs, 20p – 5p, (0.999 silver) (Edition: 1,000) .... (3)   45

Gold Sovereign Proof Sets

Many of the coins that appear in the Gold proof sets were also offered for sale as individual coins
in presentation cases with appropriate certificates. There are collectors of particular denominations
such as £2 pieces, sovereigns and half sovereigns who request coins as issued i.e. in their cases with
certificates rather than buying coins taken from sets. As a consequence, many of these individual
coins command a premium over those that might have come from cased sets. As a result the prices for
sets are often less than the sum of the individual coins.

PGS01–**1980** Gold £5 to half-sovereign (4201, 4203-4205) (Issued: 10,000)...................... (4) 2000
PGS02–**1981** U.K. Proof coin Commemorative collection. (Consists of £5, sovereign, 'Royal
Wedding' Crown (4229) in silver, plus base metal proofs 50p to ½p),
(Not known) .... (9) 1500

			£
PGS03–**1982**	Gold £5 to half-sovereign (as 1980 issue) (Issued: 2,500)	(4)	2000
PGS04–**1983**	Gold £2, sovereign and half-sovereign, (4203 – 4205) (Not known)	(3)	900
PGS05–**1984**	Gold £5, sovereign and half-sovereign, (4201, 4204 and 4205) (Issued: 7,095)	(3)	1600
PGS06–**1985**	Gold £5 to half-sovereign (4251, 4261, 4271, 4276) (Issued: 5,849)	(4)	2000
PGS07–**1986**	Gold Commonwealth games £2, sovereign and half-sovereign (4311, 4271 and 4276) (Issued: 12,500)	(3)	900
PGS08–**1987**	Gold £2, sovereign and half-sovereign (4261, 4271 and 4276) (Issued: 12,500)	(3)	900
PGS09–**1988**	Gold £2 to half-sovereign, (as 1987 issue) (Issued: 11,192)	(3)	900
PGS10–**1989**	Sovereign Anniversary Gold £5 to half-sovereign (4254, 4263, 4272, 4277), (Issued: 5,000)	(4)	4000
PGS11–**1989**	Gold £2 to half-sovereign (4263, 4272 and 4277) (Issued: 7,936)	(3)	2000
PGS12–**1990**	Gold £5 to half-sovereign (as 1985 issue), (Issued: 1,721)	(4)	2000
PGS13–**1990**	Gold £2 to half-sovereign (as 1988 issue), (Issued: 1,937)	(3)	950
PGS14–**1991**	Gold £5 to half-sovereign (as 1985 issue) (Issued: 1,336)	(4)	2000
PGS15–**1991**	Gold £2 to half-sovereign (as 1987 issue (Issued: 1,152)	(3)	950
PGS16–**1992**	Gold £5 to half-sovereign (as 1985 issue) (Issued: 1,165)	(4)	2000
PGS17–**1992**	Gold £2 to half-sovereign (as 1987 issue) (Issued: 967)	(3)	950
PGS18–**1993**	Gold £5 to half-sovereign with silver Pistrucci medal in case (Issued: 1,078)	(5)	2200
PGS19–**1993**	Gold £2 to half-sovereign (as 1985 issue) (Issued: 663)	(3)	1000
PGS20–**1994**	Gold £5, £2, sovereign and half-sovereign (4251, 4314, 4271 and 4276) (Issued: 918)	(4)	2300
PGS21–**1994**	Gold £2, sovereign and half-sovereign (4314, 4271 and 4276) (Issued: 1,249)	(3)	950
PGS22–**1995**	Gold £5,£2,sovereign and half-sovereign (4251,4315,4271and 4276) (Issued: 718)	(4)	2000
PGS23–**1995**	Gold £2, sovereign and half-sovereign (4315, 4271 and 4276) (Issued: 1,112)	(3)	950
PGS24–**1996**	Gold £5 to half-sovereign (as 1985 issue) (Issued: 742)	(4)	2000
PGS25–**1996**	Gold £2 to half-sovereign (as 1987 issue) (Issued: 868)	(3)	950
PGS26–**1997**	Gold £5,£2,sovereign and half-sovereign (4251,4318,4271 and 4276) (Issued: 860)	(4)	2000
PGS27–**1997**	Gold £2 to half-sovereign (4318, 4271 and 4276) (Issued: 817)	(3)	950
PGS28–**1998**	Gold £5 to half sovereign (4400, 4420, 4430, 4440) (Issued: 789)	(4)	2000
PGS29–**1998**	Gold £2 to half sovereign (4420, 4430, 4440) (Issued: 560)	(3)	975
PGS30–**1999**	Gold £5, £2, sovereign and half sovereign (4400, 4571, 4430 and 4440) (Issued: 991)	(4)	2000
PGS31–**1999**	Gold £2, sovereign and half sovereign (4571, 4430 and 4440) (Issued: 912)	(3)	950
PGS32–**2000**	Gold £5 to half-sovereign (as 1998 issue) (Issued: 1,000)	(4)	2000
PGS33–**2000**	Gold £2 to half-sovereign (as 1998 issue) (Issued: 1,250)	(3)	900
PGS34–**2001**	Gold £5,£2,sovereign and half sovereign (4400, 4572, 4430 and 4440) (Issued: 1,000)	(4)	2000
PGS35–**2001**	Gold £2 , sovereign and half sovereign (4572,4430 and 4440)(Issued: 891)	(3)	800
PGS36–**2002**	Gold £5 to half sovereign (4401, 4421, 4431, 4441) (Issued: 3,000)	(4)	2600
PGS37–**2002**	Gold £2 to half sovereign (4421, 4431, 4441) (Issued: 3,947)	(3)	1100
PGS38–**2003**	Gold £5 to half sovereign (as 1998 issue) (Issued: 2,050)	(4)	2000
PGS39–**2003**	Gold £2, sovereign and half sovereign (4577, 4430 and 4440) (Issued: 1,737)	(3)	900
PGS40–**2004**	Gold £5 to half sovereign (as 1998 issue) (Issued: 1,749)	(4)	2000
PGS41–**2004**	Gold £2, sovereign and half sovereign (4578, 4430 and 4440) (Issued: 761)	(3)	900
PGS42–**2005**	Gold £5 to half sovereign (4402, 4422, 4432, 4442 (Issued: 2,161)	(4)	2600
PGS43–**2005**	Gold £2 to half sovereign (4422, 4432, 4442) (Issued: 797)	(3)	1100
PGS44–**2006**	Gold £5 to half sovereign (as 1998 issue) (Issued: 1,750)	(4)	2000
PGS45–**2006**	Gold £2 to half sovereign (as 1998 issue) (Issued: 540)	(3)	1100
PGS46–**2007**	Gold £5 to half sovereign (as 1998 issue) (Issued: 1,750)	(4)	2000
PGS47–**2007**	Gold £2 to half sovereign (as 1998 issue) (Issued: 651)	(3)	900

			£
PGS48–**2007**	Gold sovereign and half sovereign (4430 and 4440) (Issued: 818)	(2)	500
PGS49–**2008**	Gold £5 to half sovereign (as 1998 issue) (Issued: 1,750)	(4)	2000
PGS50–**2008**	Gold £2 to half sovereign (as 1998 issue) (Issued: 583)	(3)	900
PGS51–**2008**	Gold sovereign and half sovereign (as 2007 issue) (Issued: 804, in addition to individual coin issues)..	(2)	500
PGS52–**2009**	Gold £5, £2, sovereign, half sovereign, and quarter sovereign (4403, 4423, 4433, 4443, and 4445) (Issued: 1,750)...	(5)	2500
PGS53–**2009**	Gold £2, sovereign and half sovereign (4423, 4433 and 4445) (Edition: 750)	(3)	950
PGS54–**2009**	Gold sovereign and half sovereign (4433 and 4443) (Edition: 1,000)............	(2)	500
PGS55–**2010**	Gold £5 to quarter sovereign (as 2009 issue) (Edition: 1,750) ....(5)		2500
PGS56–**2010**	Gold £2 to half sovereign (as 2009 issue) (Edition: 750)...................... ....(3)		975
PGS57–**2010**	Gold sovereign, half sovereign and quarter sovereign (4433, 4443 and 4445) (Edition: 1,500)..	(3)	600
PGS58–**2011**	Gold £5 to quarter sovereign (as 2010 issue) (Edition: 1,500)	(5)	3250
PGS59–**2011**	Gold £2 to quarter sovereign (4423, 4433, 4443 and 4445) (Edition: 200).....	(4)	1600
PGS60–**2011**	(Previously listed as PGS59) Gold £2 to half sovereign (as 2010 issue) (Edition: 750)	(3)	1200
PGS61–**2011**	(Previously listed as PGS60) Gold sovereign, half sovereign and quarter sovereign (4433, 4443 and 4445) (Edition: 1,000)	(3)	675
PGS62–**2012**	Gold £5, £2, sovereign, half sovereign and quarter sovereign (4404, 4424, 4434, 4444 and 4446) (Edition: 999)	(5)	3250
PGS63–**2012**	Gold £2 to quarter sovereign (4424, 4434, 4444 and 4446) (Edition: 159).....	(4)	1600
PGS64–**2012**	Gold £2 to half sovereign (4424, 4434 and 4444) (Edition: 750)	(3)	1200
PGS65–**2012**	Gold sovereign, half sovereign and quarter sovereign (4433, 4443 and 4445) (Edition: 700)	(3)	675
PGS66–**2012**	BU Gold £2 to half sovereign (4424, 4434 and 4444) (Edition: 60)...............	(3)	2000
PGS67–**2013**	Gold £5, £2, sovereign, half sovereign and quarter sovereign (4403, 4423, 4433, 4443 and 4445) (Edition: 1,000)	(5)	3600
PGS68–**2013**	Gold £2 to half sovereign (4423, 4433 and 4445) (Edition: 400)	(3)	1500
PGS69–**2013**	Gold sovereign, half sovereign and quarter sovereign (4433, 4443 and 4445) (Edition: 650)	(3)	750
PGS70–**2013**	BU Gold £2 to half sovereign (4424, 4434 and 4444) (Edition: 125).............	(3)	1550
PGS71–**2014**	Gold £5, £2, sovereign, half sovereign and quarter sovereign (4403, 4423, 4433, 4443 and 4445) (Edition: 750)	(5)	3300
PGS72–**2014**	Gold £2 to half sovereign (4423, 4433 and 4445) (Edition: 500)	(3)	1300
PGS73–**2014**	Gold sovereign, half sovereign and quarter sovereign (4433, 4443 and 4445) (Edition: 750)	(3)	625

Britannia Gold Proof Sets

PBG01–**1987**	Britannia Proofs £100, £50, £25, £10 (4281, 4286, 4291, and 4296), alloyed with copper (Issued: 10,000)	(4)	2000
PBG02–**1987**	Britannia Proofs £25, £10 (4291 and 4296) (Issued: 11,100)	(2)	450
PBG03–**1988**	Britannia Proofs £100–£10 (as 1987 issue) (Issued: 3,505)........................	(4)	2000
PBG04–**1988**	Britannia Proofs £25, £10 (as 1987 issue) (Issued: 894)...............................	(2)	450
PBG05–**1989**	Britannia Proofs £100–£10 (as 1987) (Issued: 2,268).................................	(4)	2000
PBG06–**1989**	Britannia Proofs £25, £10 (as 1987 issue) (Issued: 451)...............................	(2)	450
PBG07–**1990**	Britannia Proofs, £100–£10, gold with the addition of silver alloy (4282, 4287, 4292, 4297) (Issued: 527)..	(4)	2000
PBG08–**1991**	Britannia Proofs, as PBS07 (Issued: 509)	(4)	2000
PBG09–**1992**	Britannia Proofs, as PBS07 (Issued: 500)	(4)	2000
PBG10–**1993**	Britannia Proofs, as PBS07 (Issued: 462)	(4)	2000

£

PBG11–**1994**	Britannia Proofs, as PBS07 ((Issued: 435)...	(4)	2000
PBG12–**1995**	Britannia Proofs, as PBS07 (Issued: 500)	(4)	2000
PBG13–**1996**	Britannia Proofs, as PBS07 (Issued: 483)	(4)	2000
PBG14–**1997**	Britannia proofs £100, £50, £25, £10 (4283, 4288, 4293, 4298) (Issued: 892)	(4)	2100
PBG15–**1998**	Britannia proofs £100, £50, £25, £10 (4450, 4460, 4470, 4480) (Issued: 750)	(4)	2000
PBG16–**1999**	Britannia Proofs, as PBS15 (Issued: 740)	(4)	2000
PBG17–**2000**	Britannia Proofs, as PBS15 (Issued: 750)	(4)	2000
PBG18–**2001**	Britannia Proofs £100, £50, £25, £10 (4451, 4461, 4471, 4481) (Issued: 1,000)	(4)	2000
PBG19–**2002**	Britannia Proofs, as PBS15 (Issued: 945)	(4)	2000
PBG20–**2003**	Britannia Proofs £100, £50, £25, £10 (4452, 4462, 4472, 4482) (Issued: 1,250)	(4)	2000
PBG21–**2003**	Britannia Proofs £50, £25, £10 (4462, 4472, 4482) (Issued: 825)	(3)	800
PBG22–**MD**	Britannia BU £100 set of four different designs, 1987, 1997, 2001, 2003 (4281, 4283, 4451, 4452) (Edition: 2,500)	(4)	4000
PBG23–**2004**	Britannia Proofs, as PBS15 (Issued: 973)	(4)	2000
PBG24–**2004**	Britannia Proofs, £50, £25, £10 (4460, 4470, 4480) (Issued: 223)	(3)	850
PBG25–**2005**	Britannia Proofs, £100, £50, £25, £10 (4453, 4463, 4473, 4483) (Issued: 1,439)	(4)	2000
PBG26–**2005**	Britannia Proofs, £50, £25, £10 (4463, 4473, 4483) (Issued: 417)	(3)	850
PBG27–**2006**	Britannia Proofs, as PBS15 (Issued: 1,163)	(4)	2000
PBG28–**2006**	Britannia set of five different proof £25 designs (4470, 4471, 4472, 4473, 4474) (Edition: 250)	(5)	1500
PBG29–**2007**	(Previously listed as **PBS28**) Britannia Proofs, £100, £50, £25, £10 (4454, 4464, 4475, 4484) (Issued: 1,250)	(4)	2000
PBG30–**2008**	Britannia Proofs, £100, £50, £25, £10 (4455, 4465, 4476, 4485) (Issued: 1,250)	(4)	2000
PBG31–**2009**	Britannia Proofs, £100, £50, £25, £10 (4456, 4466, 4474, 4486) (Edition: 1,250)	(4)	2000
PBG32–**2010**	Britannia Proofs, £100, £50, £25, £10 (4457, 4467, 4477, 4487) (Edition: 1,250)	(4)	2000
PBG33–**2010**	Britannia Proofs, £50, £25, £10 (4467, 4475, 4487) (Edition: 500).................	(3)	950
PBG34–**2011**	Britannia Proofs, £100, £50, £25, £10 (4458, 4468, 4478, 4488) (Edition: 1,000)	(4)	3000
PBG35–**2011**	Britannia Proofs, £50, £25, £10 (4468, 4478, 4488) (Edition: 250)	(3)	1500
PBG36–**2012**	Britannia Proofs, as PBS15 (Edition: 550)..	(4)	3000
PBG37–**2012**	Britannia Proofs, £50, £25 and £10 (4460, 4470 and 4480) (Edition: 100).....	(3)	1500
PBG38–**MD**	Britannia Proof set of 1987 (£100 to £10, struck in copper alloyed gold, see PBS01), and set of 2012 (£100 to £10, struck in silver alloyed gold, see PBS36) (Edition: 15, sets of 1987 from the secondary market)......................	(8)	5000
PBG39–**2013**	Britannia Proofs, £100 - £1, (0.9999 gold), (4459, 4469, 4479, 4489 and 4760) (Edition: 250)	(5)	5750
PBG40–**2013**	Britannia Proofs, Premium set, £50, £25 and £10, (0.9999 gold), (4469, 4479 and 4489) (Edition: 125)	(3)	1375
PBG41–**2013**	Britannia Proofs, £25, £10 and £1, (0.9999 gold), (4479, 4489 and 4760)......	(3)	675
PBG42–**2014**	Britannia Proofs, £100 - £1, (0.9999 gold), (4459, 4469, 4479, 4489 and 4760) (Edition: 250)	(6)	2600
PGB43–**2014**	Britannia Proofs, £50 - £10, (0.9999 gold) (Edition: 100)	(3)	1175
PGB44–**2014**	Britannia Proofs, £25 - £1, (0.9999 gold) (Edition: 150)..................................	(3)	595

Gold Coin Proof Sets

PCGS1–**2002**	Commonwealth Games 'Bimetallic' £2 (4573, 4574, 4575 and 4576) in gold (Issued: 315)...	(4)	2100
PGJS1–**2002**	'Golden Jubilee' £5, 'Bimetallic' £2, 'English' £1, 50p to 1p and Maundy coins, 4p-1p, in gold proof (4555, 4570, 4594, 4610, 4630, 4650, 4670, 4212-4215) (Issued: 2,002)	(13)	5250

£

PGBNS–**2006**	'Bimetallic' 'Isambard Brunel' £2 (4581) and 'Bimetallic' 'Paddington Station' £2 (4582) gold proofs (Edition: taken from individual coin limits)	(2)	1000
PGVCS–**2006**	'Victoria Cross' 50 pence (4617), 'Wounded Colleague' 50 pence (4618) gold proof (Edition: taken from individual coin limits)...............................	(2)	975
PGBS1–**MD**	Set of four £1 coins 'Forth Rail Bridge' (4595), 'Menai Straits Bridge' (4596) 'MacNiell's Egyptian Arch' (4597) and 'Gateshead Millennium Bridge' (4598) in gold proof (Edition: 300 sets taken from individual coin limits)...........	(4)	2400
PGEBCS–**2008**	'Emblems of Britain', 'UK' £1 (4590), 'Britannia' 50 pence (4610), 20 pence to 1p gold proofs (Issued: 708)...	(7)	2600
PGRSAS–**2008**	'The Royal Shield of Arms', 'Royal Shield' £1 (4604) to 1p gold proof (4611, 4631, 4651, 4671, 4691, and 4711) (Issued: 886)	(7)	2600
PG1PCS–**2008**	Set of 14 different £1 reverse designs (4590 to 4603) (Issued: 150)	(14)	8500
PG50PCS–**2009**	Set of sixteen 50 pence reverse designs marking 40th Anniversary of the introduction of the 50 pence denomination (4610- 4625) gold proofs (Edition: 125)..	(16)	7500
PG50PPCS–**2009**	Set of sixteen 50 pence reverse designs marking 40th Anniversary of the introduction of the 50 pence denomination (4610- 4625) gold proof piedfort (Edition: 40)	(16)	20000
PGDJS–**2012**	Diamond Jubilee £5, (4569), 'Bimetallic' 'Charles Dickens' £2 (4730), 'Bimetallic' £2 (4570) 'Royal Shield '£1(4604), 50 pence to 1 pence (4620, 4631, 4652, 4672, 4691 and 4711) gold proofs (Edition: 150)....................	(10)	7000
PGCS–**2012**	Diamond Jubilee £5, (4569) and Golden Jubilee £5, (4555) (Edition: 60)..	(2)	3000
PGCS2–**2012**	Diamond Jubilee £5, (4569) and £2 (Sovereign design, 4424) set of two (Edition : 60, taken from individual coins limits)..	(2)	2600
PGCS3–**MD**	Set of six £2 with Sporting connections, Commonwealth Games 1986 (4311), European Football Championship 1996 (4317) and Commonwealth Games 2002 (4573 to 4576), coins obtained from the secondary market (Edition: 50)	(6)	3200
PGCAS–**2013**	Proof 'Coronation' £5, (4751), 'Bimetallic' 'Guinea' £2 (4731) 'Bimetallic' 'Roundel' £2 (4732), 'Bimetallic' 'Train' £2 (4733), 'Bimetallic' £2 (4570) 'Royal Shield' £1 (4604), 'England' £1 (4720), 'Wales' £1 (4721), 50 pence 'Ironside' (4628), 50 pence to 1 pence (4620, 4631, 4652, 4672, 4691 and 4711) gold proofs (Edition:60)...	(15)	11500
PGLUS–**2013**	Bimetallic 'Roundel' £2 (4732) and 'Bimetallic' 'Train' £2 (4733) gold proofs (Edition: 150)..	(2)	2000
PGQPS–**2013**	Queen's Portrait set of £5 coins, (4754 – 4757) silver proofs (Edition: 450)	(4)	9500
PG31S–**2013**	Thirtieth Anniversary set of three £1 coins, (4590, 4334 and 4604) gold proofs (Edition: 100)...	(3)	3000
PGC14–**2014**	Proof 'Queen Anne' £5, (4758), 'Bimetallic' 'Trinity House' £2 (4734), 'Bimetallic' 'World War I' £2 (4735), 'Bimetallic' £2 (4570) 'Royal Shield' £1 (4604), 'Northern Ireland' £1 (4722), 'Scotland' £1 (4723.), and 50 pence 'Commonwealth Games' (4630), gold proofs (Edition:)	(6)	

Platinum Coin **Proof sets**

PPBCS1–**2007**	Britannia Proofs £100, £50, £25, £10 (4454A, 4464A, 4474A and 4484A) (Issued: 250)..	(4)	2800
PPBCS2–**2008**	Britannia Proofs £100, £50, £25, £10 (4455A, 4465, 4476A, and 4485A) (Edition: 250)	(4)	2800
PPEBCS–**2008**	'Emblems of Britain', 'UK' £1 (4590), 'Britannia' 50 pence (4610) and 20 pence to 1p (Issued: 250)...	(7)	3500
PPRSAS–**2008**	'The Royal Shield of Arms', 'Royal Shield' £1 (4604) to 1p (4611, 4631, 4651, 4671, 4691, 4711) (Issued: 184)	(7)	3500

Pattern Proof sets   £

PPS1–**2003**	Silver proof set of £1 designs with plain edge and hallmark (4595A, 4596A, 4597A, 4598A) (Edition: 7,500)	(4)	75
PPS2–**2003**	Gold proof set of £1 designs with plain edge and hallmark (4595A, 4596A, 4597A, 4598A) (Edition: 3,000)	(4)	2300
PPS3–**2004**	Silver proof set of £1 designs with plain edge and hallmark (4595B, 4596B, 4597B, 4598B) (Edition: 5,000)	(4)	75
PPS4–**2004**	Gold proof set of £1 designs with plain edge and hallmark (4595B, 4596B, 4597B, 4598B) (Edition: 2,250	(4)	2300

LONDON 2012 OLYMPIC AND PARALYMPIC GAMES

OCNS1–**MD**	Set of 29 50 pence coins in individual card packs (4960 to 4988)	(29)	90
OCNS2	Gold Medal Winners set of 50 pence Cuni and £5 Olympic 2012 £5, (Athletics, 4960, Boxing, 4967, Canoeing, 4968, Cycling, 4961, Equestrian, 4969, Rowing, 4978, Sailing, 4979, Shooting, 4980, Taekwondo, 4982, Tennis, 4983, Triathlon, 4984 and £5, 4924) (Edition: 2,012)	(12)	45
OCNS3	Five pounds.(crowns). Set of the four Countdown issues and the Official Olympic and Paralympic £5 cuni coins. (4920 to 4925). (Edition: 2,012)	(6)	70
OCNS4	Five pounds. (crowns). Set of four Countdown issues (4920 – 4923)	(4)	45

Silver coin sets.

OSS1–**2009**.	The Mind of Britain. Set of six £5 silver proofs (4930, 4931, 4932, 4933, 4934 and 4935) (Edition: each coin 95,000)	(6)	300
OSS2–**2010**	The Body of Britain. Set of six £5 silver proofs (4936, 4937, 4938, 4939, 4940 and 4941) (Edition: each coin 95,000)	(6)	300
OSS3–**2010**	The Spirit of Britain. Set of six £5 silver proofs (4942, 4943, 4944, 4945, 4946 and 4947) (Edition: each coin 95,000)	(6)	300
OSS4–**MD**	Great British Icons. Set of 6 £5 silver proofs (4930,4931,4938,4944,4945, 4946) (Edition: 10,000 taken from individual coin limits of 95,000)	(6)	550
OSS5–**MD**	The Mind, Body and Spirit of Britain. Set of 18 £5 silver proofs (4930 to 4947)	(18)	1650
OSS6–**2011**	Set of 29 50 pence silver brilliant uncirculated coins (4960 to 4988)	(29)	900
OSS7–**2011**	Gold Medal Winners set of 50 pence silver brilliant uncirculated coins and £5 Olympic 2012 silver proof, (Athletics, 4960, Boxing, 4967, Canoeing, 4968, Cycling, 4961, Equestrian, 4969, Rowing, 4978, Sailing, 4979, Shooting, 4980, Taekwondo, 4982, Tennis, 4983, Triathlon, 4984 and £5, 4924), (Edition: 999 but coins taken from individual issue limits)	(12)	550
OSS8–**2011**	Accuracy. Set of six 50 pence silver brilliant uncirculated coins depicting various sports (Badminton, 4964, Basketball, 4965, Fencing, 4970, Football, 4971, Hockey, 4975, and Tennis, 4983) (Edition: 2,012 but taken from individual issue limits)	(6)	280
OSS9–**2011**	Agility. Set of six 50 pence silver brilliant uncirculated coins depicting various sports (Boxing, 4967, Equestrian, 4969, Gymnastics, 4973, Judo, 4976, Sailing, 4979, and Taekwondo, 4982) (Edition: 2,012 but taken from individual issue limits)	(6)	280
OSS10–**2011**	Speed. Set of six 50 pence silver brilliant uncirculated coins depicting various sports (Athletics, 4960, Aquatics, 4962, Canoeing, 4968, Cycling, 4961, Rowing, 4978, Triathlon, 4984) (Edition: 2,012 but taken from individual issue limits)	(6)	280
OSS11–**MD**	Five pounds.(crowns). Set of the four Countdown issues and the Official Olympic and Paralympic £5 proof silver coins. (4920 to 4925). (Edition: 800 taken from individual issue limits)	(6)	500

Gold coin sets.

£

OGS1–**2008**	(**Previously listed as PG2PCS**). 'Bimetallic' 'Centenary of Olympic Games of 1908' £2 (4585) and 'Bimetallic' 'United Kingdom Olympic Handover Ceremony' £2 (4951) gold proofs (Edition: 250)	(2) 1000
OGS2–**2010**	'Faster' 2-coin proof set, two £25, (4905 and 4906) (Edition: taken from individual coin Limits)	(2) 1200
OGS3–**2010**	'Faster' 3-coin proof set, £100, and two £25, (4915, 4905 and 4906) (Edition: 4,000)	(3) 3500
OGS4–**2011**	'Higher' 2-coin proof set, two £25, (4907 and 4908) (Edition: taken from individual coin limits)..	(2) 1200
OGS5–**2011**	'Higher' 3-coin proof set, £100, and two £25, (4916, 4907 and 4908) (Edition: 4,000)	(3) 3500
OGS6–**2012**	'Stronger' 2-coin proof set, two £25, (4909 and 4910) (Edition: taken from individual coin limits)...	(2) 1200
OGS7–**2012**	'Stronger' 3-coin proof set, £100, and two £25, (4917, 4909 and 4910) (Edition: 4,000)	(3) 3500
OGS8–**MD**	'Faster', 'Higher' and 'Stronger' set of three £100 (4915 – 4917) and six £25 (4905 – 4910) (Edition: 1,000 taken from individual coin limits)........	.(9)10500
OGS9–**MD**	'Countdown to London' set of four £5 gold proof coins (4920 – 4923)......	(4)11500
OGS10–**2012**	Set of £5 proof London Olympic Games and Paralympic Games (4924 and 4925) (Edition: taken from individual coin limits)	(2) 5500

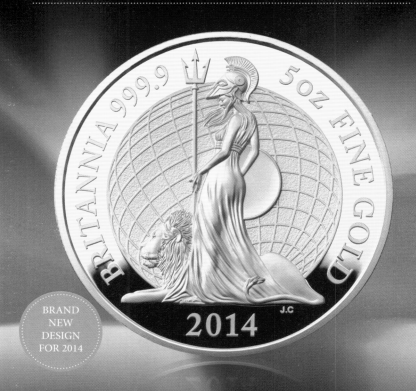